OUT
OF THE
DEPTHS

OUT
OF THE
DEPTHS

POETRY *of*
POVERTY

COURAGE *and*
RESILIENCE

EDITED BY SUSAN DEBORAH KING

Susan Deborah King

HOLY COW! PRESS
DULUTH, MINNESOTA
2015

*For Lyn, with love + the deepest gratitude
for all your help, your ebullient spirit, your
inciisivemind, and your large heart.
Always, Sam 4/5*

Cover painting: *Guiding Light* by Douglas Witmer.

Book design by Anton Khodakovsky.

Printed and bound in the United States of America.

First printing, 2015

ISBN 978-0-9859818-7-7

10 9 8 7 6 5 4 3 2 1

This project is supported in part by grant awards
from the Ben and Jeanne Overman Charitable Trust,
the Elmer L. and Eleanor J. Andersen Foundation,
the Cy and Paula DeCosse Fund of the Minneapolis
Foundation, and by gifts from individual donors.

Holy Cow! Press books are distributed to the trade by
Consortium Book Sales & Distribution, c/o Perseus
Distribution, 210 American Drive, Jackson, TN 38301.

For inquiries, please write to:
Holy Cow! Press, Post Office Box 3170,
Mount Royal Station, Duluth, MN 55803.

Visit www.holycowpress.org

"Out of the depths I cry to you, O God. O God, hear my voice! Let your ears be attentive to the voice of my supplications!"

Psalm 130

"It was nothing but walls and cold and we had to go outside to the bathroom – the roof leaking water all the time. We had what you would call a spirit that could not be killed. I didn't have toys. I started making stuff with whatever I could get my hands on."

Joe Minter, sculptor and proprietor
of the African Village in America

Introduction

A few years ago I was at my alma mater, Union Theological Seminary, to give a reading from a book of poems about my experience with breast cancer. The organization sponsoring the reading was The Poverty Initiative, a student-begun group that is a consortium of grass roots organizations around the country and abroad dedicated to the eradication of poverty. Through non-violent social action and other advocacy measures these organizations work for the betterment of life conditions for their members. I met with members of the Initiative while I was at Union and found that on a deep level we shared experiences and perspectives. By the age of 20 I had lost all my immediate family to violent death and was alienated from one member who perpetrated some of the violence. I had no home and was dependent on friends for shelter. After meeting with members of the Initiative, I began to uncover some of the shame, fear and pain that I had tried to sweep into the background since my early adulthood. I began to empathize more than I had before with the struggle of others who were in difficult and seemingly impossible situations. Yet many of them found ways by banding together to better their conditions and live more satisfying and productive lives. They have, in many cases, moved mountains of collective inertia and resistance to change laws and policies that perpetuated oppression. I was moved and inspired by many of their stories.

A study published in a recent *Atlantic Monthly* found that, proportionally, people of lesser means are more generous than those who have wealth. This finding did not surprise me based on my own experience. But what was encouraging about the study is that when those with means come in contact with those who are struggling and hear in detail about the difficulty of their lives, they are moved to compassion and generosity. Wealth can be isolating. I wondered with members of the Initiative whether poetry might be a particularly powerful way to break that isolation and the desperation engendered in those who struggle from not being heard. They agreed.

And so we entered into a partnership. I held workshops at some of their meetings of people from across the country and beyond, to generate material for the anthology. We found that the workshops themselves helped to break down some of the loneliness many of us feel when we are shut out from obtaining services, employment, health care or understanding from systems and bureaucracies not inclined to hear and address basic human need. The poems in this anthology, whether written by as-yet-unheard voices, emerging poets or poets of note, all have a cry at their center—a cry for voices of the suffering to be heard and for the dignity of those suffering to be honored. As submissions poured in, I was overwhelmed by the strength of spirit many of these poems exhibited. The souls of those who have survived the worst can sometimes be burnished beyond measure to be bright and guiding lights for those still laboring under heavy burdens. I was pained and appalled at the adversities these writers or those to whom they were connected had endured and I resonated too with some of them. I have been more acutely sensitized to the hardships experienced by people ostensibly different from myself only to find between us beneath the surface a fast connection. And I have been roused to take a more active role in promoting policies that alleviate misery and promote self-realization. May you, as readers, experience this and much more that we may not have been able to imagine, by way of edification and transformation, from reading this work.

—*Susan Deborah King, editor*
Minneapolis, 2013

With deep gratitude to Mitchell and Kate Watson
who provided funding for this project.

An Introduction

to the Poverty Initiative and the Role of Art and Culture in Building a Movement to End Poverty Led by the Poor

The Poverty Initiative, which is housed at Union Theological Seminary, brings together grassroots community and religious leaders with the mission to build a broad social movement to end poverty, led by the poor. Having identified poverty and inequality as the defining issue of our time, our work has focused on strengthening a national network of low-income, community, and religious leaders through collaborative learning, mutual support; reflection on historical and contemporary organizing; and strategic leadership. We have trained over 1,000 leaders, who make up a multi-racial, inter-generational, multi-faith, and low-income community and represent over 300 community organizations and religious congregations with proven local level successes on issues of unemployment, community revitalization, housing and homelessness, immigration, water privatization, ecological devastation, eviction and foreclosure, health care, hunger, low-wage workers rights, the organizing of poor youth, public education reform, grassroots media production, and living wages. Further, we have put on two week-long Leadership Schools, nine Strategic Dialogues and ten Study Intensives as part of our Poverty Scholars Program. Born of two remarkable legacies—the 175-year heritage of social justice ministries promoted by Union Theological Seminary and the unfinished business of the Rev. Dr. Martin Luther King, Jr.—the PI draws on four decades of organizing with and among poor US communities. The PI was founded in 2003-2004 by a group of Union students in collaboration with seminary faculty, staff and community leaders, and is charged to research and reshape public and theological debate, ministry, and social action on poverty so as to address its root causes. To address root causes and build a movement large enough, broad enough, and deep enough to change the policies and structures that create such injustice and suffering requires boldly applying what we have learned over the past decade to the dynamic challenges we face today. Therefore, in 2014, we launched a new phase of our work with two major far-reaching initiatives. The first is joining forces with the newly established Kairos: the Center for Religions, Rights and Social Justice at Union Theological Seminary. The second is creating a new Poor People's Campaign, building on the one begun by Dr. King in 1967.

Many of us—as organizers, advocates, filmmakers, artists, human rights defenders, and movement builders—have been working to break our isolation and expose the plight, fight, and insight of those most impacted by human rights violations, nationally and globally, for many decades. Leaders in this network were a part of the Break the Media Blackout Campaign that organized 3 national conferences starting in 1992 in Kansas City. Some have produced amazing documentaries of the struggles and victories of the real heroes and heroines of our society. And others have written songs for our movement including "Rich Man's House," "Up and Out of Poverty Now," and "Here We Stand." Many of us have been following in the footsteps of Rev. Dr. Martin Luther King, Jr., who organized the Poor People's Campaign in his last years, in hopes of bringing public attention to the common plight and fight of the poor across color lines and all other lines of division.

In our struggle to tell our own stories of poverty, as well as the untold stories of our movement, we recognize the indispensability of growing the work of art and culture. In a society that has the wealth and productive capacity to end poverty, we must come to realize that the continuation and growth of poverty result from a lack of political and social will to do so. As a reflection of our reality and a place where our consciousness of that reality can be reshaped, art and culture become powerful tools for moving the hearts and minds of the masses. It is in the emotive realm of art and culture that our values and beliefs are given collective meaning and expression. Art and culture are creative and dynamic components of movement building that help us to educate, empower, and build collective memory.

Our ability to build a movement to end poverty led by the poor is predicated on breaking the isolation of the poor—the growing dispossessed of this nation—and building an unsettling unity that can shake us from believing that poverty will always be with us. The urgency of this task is why we are so excited about this anthology and appreciative of the work of Susan Deborah King in coordinating it. The poems in this anthology represent not only individual stories of struggle and survival, but in their coming together build a collective memory that can reveal the contradictions of a system where poverty exists in the midst of plenty. The poems in this anthology ring out with lived experiences of poverty: we hear experiences of urgency, need, and lack in Deborah Byrne's poem, "Becoming", and "Slum Boy on Glue" by Michael Shorb; we hear cries of systemic injustice, like in "Global Inequalities" by Jayne Cortez; see images of post-industrial working class poverty, like Jim Johnson's from "Dovetailed Corners"; and hear reverent, beautiful words that sing for comfort and relief, like "Song" by Ashley Bryan.

Our expressions in these poems and the coming together of the poverty scholars who wrote them are a place where collective identity is formed and we gain strength in our movement. Crossing the boundaries of race, religion, geography, gender, and age, this collection of poetry follows the journey of what it means to be a poverty scholar and the process that we go through by telling our stories. The poems embody the lived experiences that foster our commitment to and connectedness in building a movement to end poverty. Our stories of struggle—our history—are continuously erased by dominant culture. The practice of singing, dancing, writing, quilting, and otherwise expressing these stories is a means to revive and reclaim our experience. In telling our stories we overcome the fear and disunity that are created through our isolation and give depth to our movement. If we are serious about the work of ending poverty, we must raise our voices and take back our dignity, take back our humanity. The work of art and culture gives us direction and reminds us that we are the ones we've been waiting for. Out of the depths, the spirit of our movement rises as a new and unsettling force that has the vision, the courage, and the charge to change the world.

To learn more about the Poverty Initiative and to follow us through our social media, check out our website and sign up for our e-newsletter at povertyinitiative.org.

—*Liz Theoharis*
Director, The Poverty Initiative

The Office
Colleen Wessel-McCoy

You'll need a guide to find it the first few visits
Along the pipe-filled corridors beneath the seminary
I heard MLK came through this way once

At the very end is the Poverty Initiative office
Littered with broken toys, mismatched futons, posters framed with
colored masking tape
And a blue rug clean only the first five minutes of each day

Here I learned only to worry about the things I can change
Beyond medicaid and making ends meet
To healthcare for all, real education, and the end of poverty

Table of Contents

INTRODUCTION   vii

"The Office" *by Colleen Wessel-McCoy*   xv

"The Maidservant" *by Imali Abala*   1

"Southern Summers" *by Faye Adams*   3

"Unbonded" *by Oneleilove Alston*   5

"Spic" *by Julia Alvarez*   6

"Poor House" *by Elvis Alves*   8

"Rich" *by Bobbi Arduni*   9

"Flying in Suburbia" *by Cynthia Aretz*   11

"How It Was, 1935" *by Peggy Aylesworth*   12

"Dad" *by J. Reed Banks*   14

"The New Dawn Hotel
(Life in the Shelter System)" *by Melissa Barber*   15

"Hard Times" *by Glenda Barrett*   17

"That Kind of Poor" *by Allie Marini Batts*   18

"Delaminated" *by Starr Cummin Bright*   20

"Ursus Horribilis" *by Polly Brody*   21

"Song" *by Ashley Bryan*   22

"Becoming" *by Deborah Byrne*   23

"The Wishing Well" *by Lydia Caros*   24

"Facing the Mountain" *by Deborah Brody Chen*   26

"Washing My Face" *by Sharon Chmielarz*   29

"Global Inequalities" *by Jayne Cortez*   30

"Under the Big Top" *by Mary Cowette*   32

"No New Music" *by Stanley Crouch*   33

"Factory Lives" *by Brian Daldorph*   35

"Bench Seats" *by Unglebah Daniel-Davis*   36

"We Digress" *by Ann Marie Davis*   38

"Picnic" *by Margo Davis*   43

"Broke" *by Mary Krane Derr*   45

"She Was the Kind" *by Heid Erdrich*   46

"My Cockroach Lover" *by Martin Espada*   48

"Poverty at Sixty" *by Mike Essig*   49

"Untitled" *by Amendu Evans*   51

"Dante's Inferno, 1961" *by Patricia Fargnoli*   52

"Unknown Cosmology" *by Ann Filemyr*   54

"Mining Coal" *by Deborah Finklestein*   56

"Flint, Michigan, 1955" *by Patricia Frisella*   57

"A Photo of Miners (U. S. A. 1908)" *by Brendan Galvin*   59

"Faces" *by Michael Glaser*   61

"Outside a Bar in Sioux Lookout" *by David Groulx*   62

"Time Machine, 1942" *by Meri Harary*   63

"I'm From" *by Markita Hawkins*   65

"Dream of Rebirth" *by Roberta Hill*   66

"Grieving Grandfather" *by Tanya Hough*   67

"Food Drive" *by Scott Hutchison*   70

"Karachi's Centripetal Force" *by Zehra Imam*   71

"From Dovetailed Corners" *by Jim Johnson*   72

"On Reading The Rocking Horse Winner" *by Lisa Kang*   73

"Uncle Dolan Spoke on Timbering in East Tennessee"
by Kathryn Kerr   75

"After Achieving the American Dream" *by Susan Deborah King*   76

"My Choice, Not to Ignore the Poor's Voice" *by Jonathan Langley*   78

"Wetback" *by Luis Larin*   82

"Dragon Flame Tattoo" *by James Lenfestey*   83

"A Dozen Reasons to Give Up Haggling for the
Price of Weavings" *by Roseann Lloyd*   84

"Looking at a Photograph of My Mother, Age 3"
by George Ella Lyon   85

"1/" *by Chosen Lyric*   87

"Pastor Visits Parishioner" *by Marsha Matthews*   88

"A Little Bit of Timely Advice" *by Mekeel McBride*   90

"Deluge" *by Ann McCrady*   91

"Tuesday at the Outreach Office" *by Ethna McKiernan*   92

"After My Stepfather's Death" *by Wesley McNair*   94

"Mother and Child" *by Stephen Mead*   95

"Polenta" *by Marsha Mentzer*   97

"Dedicated to the Countless South Africans
Who Gave Their Lives for Freedom and
Democracy" *by Afzal Moola*   98

"Depression Generation" *by Sharon Lack Munson*   99

"They're Coming to Take Us Away" *by Sharon Nelms*   101

"Washboard Wizard, Highland, Kansas, 1888"
by Marilyn Nelson   102

"Head Start Kids" *by Kara Newhouse*   103

"Why Shouldn't She" *by Grace Nichols*   104

"Real Estate" *by Naomi Shihab Nye*   105

"Entitlements" *by Molly O'Dell*   106

"The Beloved Is Dead" *by Gregory Orr*   107

"Posture" *by Maureen Owen*   108

"Don't Close Larry's" *by Carl Palmer*   109

"The Hyperbolist Speaks" *by Pit Menousek Pinegar*   111

"To Hope" *by Martha Postlethwaite*   115

"The Unchosen" *by David Radavich*   116

"Blood: Whose and How Much" *by Carlos Reyes*   118

"My Vision Has Rhythm" *by Lola Rodriguez*   119

"Justification of the Horned Lizard" *by Pattiann Rogers*   121

"Free Wheeling through Meffa" *by Abigail Rome*   123

"Adventure" *by Helen Klein Ross*   124

"My Name" *by Rose Schwab*   125

"Brother Sighting" *by Karen Seay*   126

"The Snow Cave Woman" *by Anne E. Seltz* 127

"'Escape' Artist" *by Gene Severson* 128

"Pink Slip" *by Betsy Sholl* 129

"Slum Boy on Glue" *by Michael Shorb* 131

"First of the Month Kool-Aid" *by Marty Silverthorne* 133

"Bountiful" *by Claudia Solotaroff* 135

"Bar" *by Aaron Stauffer* 137

"What a Wake-Up Call" *by Madreen Stevens* 138

"Ballad" *by Tony Stoneburner* 140

"Trouble, Fly" *by Susan Marie Swanson* 143

"Ten Gallons of Tough" *by Tiffany Tate* 144

"The War is Over" *by John Thiemeyer* 145

"Scribe" *by Kim Tran* 147

"Self-Employment, 1970" *by Natasha Trethewey* 148

"Street Wise" *by Conne Walle* 149

"Gone" *by Beverly Welsh* 150

"Lakeview Lounge" *by John Wessel-McCoy* 151

"Little Tree" *by Daniel Williams* 153

"Witness" *by Tony Voss Williams* 155

"Desert Cenote" *by Keith Wilson* 158

"Namesake" *by Laura Madeline Wiseman* 159

"Spokane Reservation School Teacher: Wellpinit, Washington"
by Carolyne Wright 160

"Jairus's Daughter" *by Pam Wynn* 161

"Hindu Prayer" *by Anu Yadov*   162

"Painting Angels" *by Jane Yolen*   166

"The Escape Artist" *by Kevin Young*   167

"What Helps" a group poem
by the Wendell E. Patrick Fun(k)ology Hour   169

Notes on Contributors   171

Permissions and Sources   192

About the Editor   193

The Maidservant
Imali Abala

I quit my job today—
    It was the best decision I ever made,
    The first time ever I used my mind
    What an exhilarating feeling!
    Never again shall I be a dishrag
    To that fat-pot-bellied nit wit, disease-infected
    Beer-stinking, tobacco-chimney boss of mine

I quit my job today—
    It was the best decision I ever made!
    Never again shall I listen to my mistress's nagging—
    Scolded without cause
    Humiliated without reason
    Starved without mercy
    What a debilitating experience.

I quit my job today—
    It was the best thing I ever did!
    Never again shall I suffer my mistress's indignity
    For she laughed at me
    Pointed a finger at me
    As though I were scum
    A cow-dung imbecile without brains
    "Don't ever lament to me you filthy wench
    You stinking goat from Kakamega!"
    So I hang my head in shame.

I quit my job today—

    It was the most liberating decision I ever made.

    Never again shall I be scorned by my mistress!

    As I near the end rope of my life,

    I, daughter of woman, have suffered the injustice of life.

    For poverty had robbed me of an education.

    For poverty had robbed me of the joy of youth,

    Sodomized at the hand of my pot-bellied

    Beer-stinking, good-for-nothing boss of mine

    For poverty had robbed me of happiness

    For poverty had robbed me of life

    Infected with HIV at the tender age of 15

    Now death smiles at me with open arms,

    As wide as the eyes can see, to receive me.

    I have no choice in the matter

    Just as much as I had none in life.

So I quit my job today—

    It was the most liberating thing I ever did.

    As I walked out of my mistress's house,

    I raised my eyes up into the depth of sky,

    Fluffy clouds like cotton balls glided with ease

    To a whirr of sober birds unlike my world's gloom.

    To the browned, zinc-tainted roof tops

    Of an unwelcoming city that looked like a wasteland,

    Of a dead past like the dreams of my formative years.

    So I close my eyes, sealing my fate forever

    Ending a life lived in disharmony.

Southern Summers
Faye Adams

A two-story house stands silent,
no longer prideful of its bay window,
running water in the kitchen,
and shower in the basement,
or of having erased memories
of shotgun houses with no heat
and backyard water pumps.

Its blank windows stare
onto fields where cotton once grew
tall and green; where stinging dirt clods
flew from our brother's straight arm,
whose aim my sister and I could never match.

Its closed face once laughed
at red noses, dust-crusted necks, muscles
tightening under skin worn wax paper thin
by twelve-hour days under burning skies
and the bitter taste of ashes
blown in by a greedy little weevil.

Our minds hung heavy
with hard-packed dirt and skimpy crops
as our hoes wielded strength and hope,
our toil fueled by dreams

of emerald fields and rain-kissed rows,
our memories ripe with younger days
when we swam in creeks, bucketed
minnows and climbed trees
in search of possum grapes.

Unbonded
Oneleilove Alston

I must learn again to bond
after losing my first friend, sibling and wombmate.
I must learn again to trust
after feeling abandoned from day one.
I must learn again to share
after losing the first person I ever shared
food, water, and shelter with.
I must learn again to light the flame of love
after my twin flame was snuffed out.
How can I mourn a loss that was so early?
How can I mourn the loss of someone only Mother and I knew?
Silence suffocates.
I am grateful for all I have today
but I still feel that someone has been missing.
I need to cry 30-year-old tears.
If we had been home in a Yoruba village
we would have been given a healing ritual and divine guidance
but we lived in the ghetto, so loss was expected.
At least the Black male would not know
the pain of *stop and frisk*, hustling and gun shots.
He would die eventually, so why not today?
There was no ritual, no tears, no village to raise us;
one on earth and the other in ancestor land.
No knowledge that there is no separation
between the living and the dead.
Just my mother's silent tears
and my unspoken fear that I won't ever be able to bond again.

Spic
Julia Alvarez

Out on the playground, kids were shouting, *Spic*!
lifting my sister's skirts, yanking her slip.
Younger, less sexy, I was held and stripped
of coat and book bag. Homework tumbled out
into oncoming traffic on the street.
Irregular verbs crumpled under tires
of frantic taxis, blew against the grates
of uptown buses we would later take
when school let out, trailed by cries of *Spic*!

That night when we asked Mami, she explained:
our classmates had been asking us to *speak*,
not to be so unfriendly, running off
without a word. "This is America!
The anthem here invites its citizens
to speak up. *Oh see, can you say*," she sang,
proving her point, making us sing along.
She winked at Papi, who had not joined in
but bowed his head, speaking of God instead:
"Protect my daughters in America."

I took her at her word: I raised my hand,
speaking up during classes, recess time.
The boys got meaner. *Spic ball*! they called out,
tossing off my school beanie, playing catch
while I ran boy to boy to get it back.

They sacked my stolen lunch box for their snacks,
dumping the foreign things in the garbage bin,
Spic trash! But I kept talking, telling them
how someday when I'd learn their language well,
I'd say what I'd seen in America.

Poor House
Elvis Alves

Father sits in the living room,
a sad look on his face
as he stares at empty walls.

Mother is in the kitchen cooking
rice in a pot whose lid becomes
undone, spilling
starch-infused water
all over the stove.
She stares but does not notice
the volcano-like eruption.

Sister is in her room
crying as her boy child
runs wild wearing a soiled
diaper.
His father beats her
and the more she loves him.

Brother is away in prison,
modern day slave ship built
for people who look like
him.
His sons roam the streets
One day they too will
follow him there.

Who am I? The narrator.
The other.

Rich
Bobbi Arduni

When the bread truck came
       at 5 AM
pulling up to the Italian grocery
       in the hush of predawn New York winter
       suburban mountains of snow
         piled high in parking lot mounds,
the gas from the exhaust
       matched our cigarette smoke,
       matched the puffs of our heavy breaths
         as we blew warm air on our own
         red-chapped fingers
          in our poor man's gloves—
           thumb holes cut into the sleeves of our
           black sweatshirts
           quarter-sized holes cut with a butterfly knife.

We'd walked for hours
       trying to stay warm.
         Waiting.
And those hours—1:30 to 5 AM—stretched
       on for
           d   a   y   s

We walked Main Street,
       hiding from the police
       ducking behind bushes
         alleyways and dumpsters
         abandoned buildings and snowy parks,

holding hands,
telling stories,
singing the city into existence.

When the bread truck came,
   it dropped off hard rolls and loaves
   wrapped in plastic on stacked trays,
     then pulled away,
       trusting.
We dashed out of the alleyway
   ripped open a bag, grabbed four hard rolls.
I stuffed one into my mouth,
   felt the soft dough on my tongue and teeth,
     felt rich and clever and invincible.
I wanted to stay that way forever.

Flying in Suburbia

Cynthia S. Aretz

Pig tails and skinned knees, I would search
the jungles of suburbia
for a wounded butterfly, a birdlet
who couldn't fly, grasshopper
with no hop, motherless mice.

My young heart and pudgy hands reached out,
clutching my prize, knowing I could give comfort,
healing to my winged and fragile friends.

Sliding out of bed on footed jammies
I checked on my patients.
Amid the screaming, dish-breaking, door-slamming,
that was my other world.
Peace and freedom were in those jars,
song and freedom in that cage.

Remember me, I would whisper.
Come back for me,
when I had to release them to Mother Nature.

I think of butterflies when I'm called
"less-than."
I remember wings beating, the wind
rising to the sky.

How It Was, 1935
Peggy Aylesworth

Sunday supper
was no different
except for buttered rye.
I watched them talk
into their plates.
My uncle, bowed,
had lost his prayer,
his thunder thinned to gray,
bits clinging to his buttoned vest,
waiting for events
that had already happened.
He'd built a house for her in Newark,
Mediterranean and high-terraced.
She learned of loss and profit
reading tiny figures'
in the daily paper,
pleased with reports
from children
safe at Vassar, Princeton.

New York City, fifth floor walk-up,
might have been
just one more change of rooms,
except for nightly roaches.
In the yellow kitchen light

enameled porcelain table
with its corner nicked to black
my eyes took refuge
as I ate
the buttered sisal bread,
my secret taste...
the dark, wet turnings of my tongue,
slightly sour, rough.
I'd look out the window
at the moon as they
complained of Roosevelt
and his socialist ideas.
After supper, soapy water
puckered up my fingers.
In the living room they gathered
at the radio and listened
to Jack Benny. I never
heard them laugh out loud.

Dad
J. Reed Banks

When I was nine, he bought the *World Book Encyclopedia*, on
installment, from the two young men in white shirts and ties working
our street door to door. It's for you, he said. It has everything there is
to know, he said. He said it with certainty and no little pride, with that
purse of lip that always betrayed to me his unabashed self-satisfaction.
Even then, though I knew better...
poised as I was to be suspect of most of his promises—
even then, how could I spoil his complete giving....
wrapping it as he did—all the world's knowledge—in this bequest,
though he himself could not read a word of it.
Here in poverty of word and resource he bequeathed to me his
package of mystery bought with his toil at a dollar fifteen an
hour. Gratitude comes after the fog of white shirts and ties: He
gave what he could, more than he could, what even the poorest
of us may hold and give, indeed, everything there is to know.

The New Dawn Hotel
(Life in the Shelter System)
Melissa Barber

Did you hear about the babies who were bitten
by rats in their cribs last night?
Or the walls saturated with mold, causing
chronic asthma in our children?
Did you hear about the many families who received
on $16 per month of food stamps
to feed themselves?
Did you hear about the ceilings caving or the leaky
pipes or the broken boiler that never
gets addressed—
because they've found a better way to ignore and silence the poor?
Did you hear about the family who almost got
burned to a crisp because the caseworker
gave them a faulty-wired heating system after
management refused to repair the boiler
or the radiator in the freezing temperatures?
Did you hear about the babies being dumped
because their parents cannot feed them?
Did you meet the ten new families that became
homeless last week because their homes
were foreclosed?
Did you see the little baby who was so fragile, starved
and dehydrated, because her parents
couldn't afford food or milk?

So,
How could you not fight for a better world?
How could you not pray for the assurance of faith?
Or hope for every tear to be wiped away?

Hard Times
Glenda Barrett

Poverty was all I could see in the photo.
Grandmother's loosely fitting clothes,
worn boards on the house, tattered chairs
sprawled on the front porch.

How odd I'd never felt poor before,
even though I lived the same way.
I'd heard Mamma say, I cried one day
for a can of hairspray.

I have no memory of it.
Does that mean it didn't affect me,
or did I learn to quit asking for things,
knowing the answer would be the same?

Grandma didn't have that gaunt look
like some folks during the Depression,
but a determined look on her face from
rearing seven children alone in hard times.

Not once in her lifetime did I see her cry.
I wonder if we were like the old saying
I've heard many times in the country.
You don't miss what you've never had.

That Kind of Poor
Allie Marini Batts

We are that kind of poor
that never really realizes how poor we are

only that the bank account hovers treacherously close to zero
in the days leading up to payday

sometimes it occurs to us that
maybe not everybody has the lights turned off
sometimes
because they're over a month behind and can never time
that three-paycheck month just right to finally catch up

or that not everyone considers more than $50 for groceries
extravagant
or clips
coupon
after coupon
that never feel like they actually help
all that much

or feels grateful that $11 an hour with two college degrees
is the best pay they've ever gotten
so what if the insurance is too expensive to afford
it's available, at least

making too much money to get food stamps
and too little to do anything but juggle the bills and pray
working longer hours and more odd jobs than we ever expected
but never thinking it's all that strange because

everyone we know
is right here with us

sinking
day
by
d
a
y

Delaminated
Starr Cummin Bright

Coming apart,
Not just at the seams
But entirely.
The exterior hull
Dried and cracked,
Lies detached,
A fragile husk.

Tacking and brads
Pulled away by the force of contraction—
Every makeshift method
You tried to use
To keep up appearances–
Gone.

The epoxy itself,
That skin binding glue,
Peels in the sun,
Brown and flaked.
What you thought
Was holding it all together,
Had no substance.

The true interior,
The guts of being,
Lies naked,
For anyone who still cares,
To pick up the pieces.

Ursus Horribilis
Polly Brody

The bear has been trying the cache again,
Mother's voice, high and anxious.
We have to get out there now,
before this late afternoon sun quenches
behind the black spruce hill-line,
before dusk makes all approaches dreadful.
We must take up the weathered boards
and smear our lamp-black under them,
masking again the scent of edible treasure
stored in that root cellar.

Out in our dimming yard,
we kneel at the hatch,
lifting screws—
four on her side, four on mine.
The lid comes free,
we hurry with black paste,
smearing the tarp over our cache.

I can feel the bear gathering itself
from the dark pooling between trees,
swaying there, head down.
We stay, backs vulnerable,
until the last screw is twisted home.
That grizzly, humped dreadnought,
detaches from the forest,
shadowing toward us.

Song
Ashley Bryan

Sing to the sun
It will listen
And warm your words
Your joy will rise
Like the sun
And glow
Within you

Sing to the moon
It will hear
And soothe your cares
Your fears will set
Like the moon
And fade
Within you

Becoming
Deborah Byrne

oh, she's becoming a crazy lady.
a big, fat crazy lady with dyed black hair
& blissful red lips, who says pizzle
to all questions asked. Her hair is most
times set in spongy pink curlers
& she wears slippers (the kind that are
animals, but you can't tell what kind
because she's ripped the heads off). yes,
she's becoming
a crazy lady, with sleeves
held onto the bodice of her dress
by safety pins & slippers (again),
on the wrong feet 'cause she drinks
too much peppermint schnapps. her travels
take her to beacon hill, where she hums
to the moon in front of rich peoples' houses.
on her days off, she holds
court in central square, barks
with dogs & does the naughty
shimmy. she wears foils on her head
because aliens need a landing spot
& she's it. late at night
in the rooming house, she sets
up twenty-five mirrors, strikes
a greta garbo pose, imagines
a jungle,
just after it rains.

The Wishing Well
Lydia Caros

If I gave
everything I have
until my last breath
there would
still be suffering
everywhere.
Women, young children,
elders, innocent animals
sick and wandering
and hungry.
No matter
where I look,
they are there.
I try to help
and yet
there are so many
I feel frustrated
and desperate
and tempted to
rail against God
(knowing it's not
God's department).
Whose department is it?
The manager's been on vacation
for more than a millennium;

and the voice mail is full.
In the lobby
there's a wishing well
filled with coins
of all the others
who've been here to ask.
I toss in the coins I have today
and head for the elevator.

Facing the Mountain
Deborah Brody Chen

His inculcation came from his father
Not his mother.
It wasn't being tied to a bedpost as a toddler
That did it—
In that home that was also a sawmill.
It was the father
Who gambled compulsively
Lost two houses worth of livelihood
And routinely threatened to trade in his mother
For two nineteen-year-olds
With no glass eye between them
While she made ends meet on
Money he didn't bring home,
And a third grade education.
Ran the shop
Kept the accounts
Cooked five meals a day and treaded out the black water
In the great tubs
Of clothes
For eighteen laborers;
Raised two children
In the chronic uncertainty
And the gangsters coming to
Flip over the dining room table
Cursing
How dare you eat if you
Don't pay us first?

His inculcation came from his father
Not his mother.
But her swallowed pain
Did ripple
Ceaselessly
Through the bonds of mother to child
Poisoning
Pitting sibling against sibling
Until
In classic inversion
He blamed women as his abusers
And
Repeated his father's theogony
On me.
Compulsively spent
Two houses worth of livelihood
On books
And stock market black holes.
Such subtle rhymes
Made the reason,
Kept us precarious
Kept him 'under pressure'
Too tired and tight
To touch his wife or his children
Yes, addiction served
Justified the neglect and belittling
The reassigning of
Reality.
Naming woman the
Oppressor
Castrator
Kept me gentle,

Turned down two careers
To tend to his instead.
Inherited his mother's grief,
Kept peace
Soothed tempers
Raised two children
Alone.
Held the shadow on my back
But fire in my chest
To light their way out.
Incense
At the altar of their ancestors.
Today
They are grown.
And I
Am walked far enough
Away from the karma mountain
To turn around,
To see it
From plain to peak.
And back again.

Washing My Face
Sharon Chmielarz

This morning when I cupped my hands to rinse my face,
when I lifted them, eyes closed,
the image they carried
up out of nowhere, out of the water, after all these years,
that same old thing,
my father, bent over,
beating my mother: her twisted face. Bent over
the sink, hands dripping, I waited
for the scene to pass, all the while shaking.
That this can keep coming up.
That this can keep coming up.
That my own hands keep bringing it up
out of the well.

Global Inequalities
Jayne Cortez

Chairperson of the board
is not digging for roots
   in the shadows
There's no dying-of-hunger stare
   in the eyes of
Chief executive officer of petroleum
Somebody else is sinking into
   spring freeze of the soil
Somebody else is evaporating
   in the dry wind of the famine
there's no severe drought
   in the mouth of
Senior vice president of funding services
No military contractor is sitting
   in the heat of a disappearing lake
No river is drying up
   in the kidneys of
   minister of defense
Under-secretary of interior
   is not writing distress signals
   on shit house walls
Do you see a refugee camp cooped up
   in the head of
Vice president of municipal bonds
There's no food shortage
   in the belly of
   a minister of agriculture

Chief economic advisors are
   addicted to diet pills
Banking committee members are
   suffering from obesity
Somebody else is sucking on dehydrated nipples
Somebody else is filling up on fly specks
The Bishops are not
   forcing themselves to eat bark
The security exchange commission members
   are sick from
   too many chocolate chip cookies
The treasury secretary
   is not going around in circles
   looking for grain
There's no desert growing in the nose of
   Supreme commander of justice
It's somebody else without weight
without blood without land
It's somebody else
Always somebody else

Under the Big Top
Mary Cowette

I locked my bedroom door. My door. It
showed the damage from being beat on,
kicked in. Brown splinters. Outside I
could hear the chaos. Inside my
bedroom played circus music. Pink
flowered curtains blew in the wind. I sang.
I danced. I dressed up. My dolls, my bears
were my audience. They cheered. They
smiled. They loved me. Under my big top
of purple green and orange, I was safe.

No New Music
Stanley Crouch

In Mississippi
balloons of hunger
blow themselves up
in the bellies of
children on porches
      in slat-thin houses
held up by stilts,
the teeth of mad
men turned to wood
to wood and tar paper
and holes in the roof
         "Holy vessel of truth
sail through the night now and save these children
these children whose legs bend bowed under the
bone-wilting fire of rickets"

Black Queen
empty as a raped peanut shell,
lie down beneath your quilt
of roaches and pray for your children
pray to the stars who
spy at night on your poverty
on your husband with his arm
across his eyes
his hands smooth with no money and no work nowhere

his eyes tattooed with the
red neck and face
of the devil himself,
his eardrums playing
back the tunes of abuse
the beasts blow through
their corncob pipes…

                No new music

Factory Lives
Brian J. Daldorph

We lived by the factory
that was killing my Dad:
his cough wouldn't get better–
"Smoke Lung," we called it.

My Dad hated the work,
did overtime so I wouldn't have to do it,
so he could send me to schools
where I'd learn things
he didn't have a clue about,
but respected.

He'd touch my schoolbooks
like they were holy:
"Get all this in your head
and you won't have to do factory work."
Home from college
I'd get up same time as my Dad,
and I'd hit the books.

I'd watch him trudge off
down the front path
in the shadows of chimneys
spewing out burnt-up lives
as black smoke
into the hard, white sky.

Bench Seats
Unglebah Daniel-Davis

I keep you in the back of my throat
like works I used to know
or like the scent of chemical solvent
and cigarette smoke
when I helped you
rebuild the engine,
cleaning bolts in the sink
in brown liquid like lung water.
I held my breath then,
turning my head towards the door.
Now I breathe into my hands
to refresh my memory,
inhaling air trapped in warm palms,
blowing on glass again,
cutting the shape of your face into the frost,
erasing it with my breath,
like I did when my hot fingers
doodled stick figures of a girl and boy
on the passenger window
you installed so I would stay warm
that April, riding next to you,
in a snow storm, driving
through Flagstaff to Vegas
without a heater or windshield wipers.

Baby, my love for you is a lopsided cart,
a broken-down Ford, this old '54
that got us there and back,
but I'm still lost on the side of the road,
thumb out, hoping,
trying to glue my wheels back together,
digging in the dirt for every piece I've lost,
blowing on my hands again for warmth.

We Digress
Ann Marie Davis

We went
to dinners
with our lovers
and we talked
on our cell phones
to our colleagues
even though
we did not like them
but we talked
to make our money
to buy gadgets
that we needed
but did not need
but that drove
our economy
that kept us
in our jobs
we came to hate
but that paid
our health insurance
that paid
for our cures
for our ailments
that we got
from our going
to our jobs
that wore us out

that paid us
to pay our mortgages
for our houses
just for us
to come home to
and then leave from
and then go back to
from our jobs
that we kept
to buy cars
we loved to drive
and sit in traffic
that we hated
but we drove
to the jobs
we tried to leave
but which paid
for the tab
for our dinners
we did not finish
with our lovers
we did not talk to
on vacations
that we went to
to unwind
from the jobs
we longed to leave
to sit in houses
we longed to leave
for vacation homes
that we left
for outings

that we left
for phone calls
that we ended
to attend charity dinners
to save our ozone
and the children
in the war zones
we destroyed
with our battles for our gas
for our cars
that we drove
because we loved them
that we bought
because we loved them
and stayed inside them
when we were frightened
of the people
who were out there
who were homeless
when it was clear
we did not want them
as our neighbors
when it was clear
that they were
the kind of people
we did not want
to brush up against

to stand next to
in our lives
when it was clear
they were the ones

we ran away from
to the suburbs
that we drove from
to the cities
that we went to
for the jobs
that we left
when we went
to the vacations
to the places
where the people
did not like us
because we were
so USA
and so we cried
like little children
when our soldiers
were returned
back to our arms
or to their graves
in little pieces
after fighting
for our oil
for our gas
for our cars
so we could drive
in our cars
to our bars
and movie theatres
to our malls
with air conditioning
to escape

from the heat
to escape
from our lives
to escape
from ourselves
to escape
the hot summers
that we got
from our driving
in our cars
from our suburbs
to our jobs.

Picnic
Margo Davis

My brother fishtailed along the gravel,
he and Dad debating the perfect tree
along the lake, until Dad yelled, *HERE.*
As they untied the trunk, my new friend
and I lined up like leaf ants to pass
fried chicken, potato salad, flaky biscuits,
and an icy watermelon which kept
Dad's cold beer upright in the cooler.
Each barked conflicting orders as we giggled
behind fanned-out hands, rolled our eyes.
My birthday cake above our heads,
we swiped a dollop of gooey chocolate
until one of us dropped it—icing first—
in the coarse stones crunching underfoot.
We froze as if hearing, *Simon Says.*
When my brother raised his hand
to lop off pebbled icing, blessing the cake
like Father McGregor, we giggled in relief.
Dad cursed, muttering, *wasted store-bought,*
adding to his list: *double night shift,*
damn kids—then paused to look
across the lake as if our mother would
float back. He refused to eat with us
as he downed beer, all those bottles
falling and rolling along the grass

and then he bowled our melon at the tree,
its trunk only slowing the inevitable
plop into the lake before splitting
into two halves which bobbed before
going around the bend. My brother took off
on foot, disappearing. Dad veered home
as we pouted in the back seat
over our loss—cake, watermelon.

Broke

Mary Krane Derr

Over the burst yellowed futon
the shutoff fan of 4 blades
perennially minus 1
give the bold outstretching shadow
of that giant Jesus in Rio.

She Was the Kind
Heid Erdrich

She was the kind
To tell it like it is
To kiss and tell
To kiss and kill
To kill with kindness

She was the kind
To get things through her thick skull
To work her fingers to the bone
To work on her back
To never take lying down

She was the kind
To lay down the law
To get down on her knees
To get up on her feet
To give an inch and take a mile

She was the kind
To stand up for herself
To sit down strike
To go to the wall
To take it to the limit

She was the kind
To take it too far
To drop off the face of the earth
To face the music
To hit rock bottom

She was the kind
To get back on that horse and ride it
To get up on her high horse
To get down to business
To turn the world upside down

My Cockroach Lover
Martin Espada

The summer I slept
on JC's couch,
there were roaches
between the bristles
of my toothbrush,
roaches pouring
from the speakers
the stereo.
A light flipped on
in the kitchen at night
revealed a Republican
National Convention
of roaches,
an Indianapolis 500
of roaches.

One night I dreamed
a giant roach
leaned over me,
brushing my face
with kind antennae
and whispering, "I love you."
I awoke slapping myself
and watched the darkness
for hours, because I realized
this was a dream
and so that meant
the cockroach
did not really love me.

Poverty at Sixty
Mike Essig

Poverty is the fence around your life. Poverty wakes you up at 4 AM
only to whisper meaningless slogans in your ear. It is the school of
piranha nibbling at the back of your brain. It is two hours waiting in
the anteroom of despair for $22 worth of food stamps and being glad
to be there. It is changing your phone number frequently because bill
collectors are such boring conversationalists. It is the empty space
your heels used to fill. It is letting your hair grow long and scraggly and
your grizzled beard sprout because you know that although you sleep
in a rented room tonight, the street is not far off, and you want to fit in
when you arrive. Poverty scalds the lint from your pockets. It is your
private Treblinka within which you rage but are crushed. It is desperate
prayers against dental catastrophes, blown tires, surprises of any sort.
Poverty is when everything you own is frayed including your nerves
from sleepless moments spent trying to solve the equation that will
make X number of dollars cover X +? amount of bills, knowing that
such math would defeat Newton or Einstein. Poverty is eying the cat's
kibble imagining that with a bit of sugar and a splash of milk it might
be fine and then eyeballing the cat himself thinking of protein of last
resort and trying not to measure him against the microwave door. You
ration your cigarettes; whiskey is a fading memory. Passing a diner on
the street, you catch a whiff of burgers too expensive to consider and
experience a Pavlovian moment. Poverty is trying to keep your head
up and remembering you pawned your neck. Poverty is watching the
needle eat your last few gallons of gas. Poverty is the archaeology of
despair. It portends the death of irony. There is nothing ironic about
a car with 217,000 miles and no insurance on it. Facts are facts in the
world of poverty. Poverty is the last quarter reclaimed from beneath

the cushions. It is too much time and not enough quarters. It is the specious logic of the self-righteous proclaiming that you deserve to be poor because you are, which, in America, passes for wisdom. Poverty makes each day like the next because nothing does not vary. It is who you are and where you are going, although you won't get far. It is the life you lead inside the fence. It is the sum of what you lack. It just is.

[Untitled]
Amendu Evans

When I was young, my mother used to work
for a store that served food,
and sometimes she would not even get paid.
They would give her food
to take home for her eight kids
but no money.
And that kind of made me understand
about the need for
a union job and its benefits.

Dante's Inferno
1961
Patricia Fargnoli

I walked in to the blast of bump and grind.
A stripper in blue light was jiggling the yeasty dough
of her breasts in the face of the front-table guy.
He was there in back, clouded in cigar smoke,
just as I'd feared, drinking strega with five pisans.
Beneath my black maternity sweater our third child
thumped in my belly. He hadn't come home;
he never came home. It was 1 AM. I was twenty-three.
I left the children sleeping. Left them!
I would have escaped if I'd known how—
no skills, no family, his dollars gone to ale,
the horses. Coronet Brandy.
Poverty. We lived it. The stove repossessed,
the cheap sectional worn through to foam.
More than forty years later I can barely say this.
He wouldn't leave the club. I begged him. He ignored me.
So I sat alone at an adjoining table
in the crowd of tables. Big Al and The Count
har-harring, as my husband, showing off, slid a dollar
from his suit pocket and lit it.
My eyes filled as the flame rose from his silver Ronson
to the bill, its fire curling
toward me, a tongue flicking, as if
the devil himself was teasing.
I breathed in its acridness; what could I do against this?

Nothing. I did nothing.
He's dead. The children near fifty. What stays?
That fire curling toward me; it still curls toward me.
I want to shriek at them: Chips, Big Red, Mike the Prince,
all of them, want to yank what is left
out of the burning air as if it is one dollar for milk,
one dollar for bread, one dollar for rent,
one small necessary dollar.

Unknown Cosmology

Ann Filemyr

Dogs growl. Cats purr.
The double blade of the can opener
dents the soup can. The rusted handle sticks.
Worn out metal teeth barely grip the lid.
We're hungry and dig the thick goo out
 trying not to cut our fingers on the jagged lip.
One baby tooth beneath the pillow. Praying for fairies
to leave their pot of gold, the little hoarders
hiding what we want the rut of rainbows.
Half moon shines in daylight
like a cracked quarter in the crowded sky.
We three hide in the highest branches
of the backyard climbing tree
our bellies rumbling
trying to stay free from trouble.
Supper is late. No lunch.
The interior gods of the house
determine these things
which we mere mortal children
have no control over. That's when
a gigantic green meteor
streaks down practically hitting
the neighbor's house, a boiling ball
of lime fire. We freeze, point, mouths
gasping like fish in dead air. No one sees it.
But us, shaking in the dusk of that trailing star.

Dinner! Mother God hollers out the back door.
Father God stomps out the front
the belch of his backfire
his tires spitting gravel
blue chicory blooming
in the ditch beside the fox tail.

Mining Coal
Deborah Finklestein

Remove darkness
from the earth,
keep some for
myself, store
it in my lungs to
keep it safe.
Watch the light
of the canary,
keep it alive
and pray the rabbit stays
alive too—there are no more seats
at my table. Dine on black
beans and a teaspoon of butter,
The only light
in my home shines
from between my wife's legs.
Keep her womb dark.
Keep my family fed.
Keep myself safe.
Balance the light
and the dark.

Flint, Michigan. 1955
Patricia Frisella

We could smell them coming with their hot tar
and flaming torches, gathered in a seething mob
suspicion dropping from their lips. We fled to hide
in walls and under beds. They dragged
us out by the hair from our warrens.

Aliens, we had broken the law and order
of their lives, our presence among them as welcome
as a heathen horde galloping down from the steppes
to rape and vanish without a trace.

Leaving no lasting marks, we float over neon
signs and billboards, failing to conform
to advertised norms, to pass as American.

With our bells of holey socks and hand-me-downs
we are welcome as lepers in the walled city, a blight of pearls
among swine rattling white eviction papers.
We are hungry enough to eat acorns.

We land in new spots where old ladies
sew pinafores and petticoats, sisters of mercy
pass along rag bags of shirts and blouses
smelling of naphtha, moth balls or sweat.

Constant ejections scatter castaways
disposable people, the dispossessed

Palestinians, Armenians, Biafrans, displaced
peoples with their misplaced children
their trails of tears, their tales of enclosures.

We weep and retreat and forget all we left behind
in the amnesia of the alien. Landlords put up For Sale signs.
Smokestacks decay. The hunting's no good in this town
of crummy schools and no jobs. We are gypsies
mumbling backward through time, limping toward oblivion.

Hinted at in headlines, the War on Poverty
becomes a war on the poor—Let us make it illegal
to hit the skids, be badly bred or different.
See how simply they smile, how badly they smell.
They build their temples and markets in the dust of our bones.

A Photo of Miners
(USA, 1908)

Brendan Galvin

With trees backing them
instead of the pit's mouth,
they could have been
a fifth grade picnic.
But the spit baller won't grow into
his father's jacket, and a ladder
of safety pins climbs the front of
the class clown. Stretch
who got tall the soonest
has the air of a chimney sweep,
and here is a little grandfather
in brogans and rag gloves,
his face shoved between two shoulders
his arms are draping,
his eyes flashing the riding lights
of pain. They are a year's
supply, average age, give or take
a year: ten. Don't look for
a bare foot at a devil-may-care
 angle on one of the rails,
or a habitable face for a life
you might have led— that
mouth is rigid as a mail slot,
the light on those hands predicts

common graves. Does anything transcend
the walleyed patience of beasts,
the artless smirk on the boy
with the high forehead
who thinks he will croon his way
out of this?

Faces
Michael Glaser

"God is resident in all faces."
—*Abraham Joshua Heschel*

God challenges our faith
with the face of poverty,

brings us to the altar
of our own emptiness

and asks us if we have the courage
to look at this

and bear witness.

Outside a Bar in Sioux Lookout
David Groulx

Outside a bar in Sioux Lookout there
is an Indian man selling his paintings
They will be worth something someday, but not today

Today they are worth a bottle of wine

Today they are worth
Queen Elizabeth's silver tea set

Today they are worth the first stone
thrown at Mary Magdalene

Today they are worth the night
the angel entered Mary
and Joseph never knew

Today they are worth the night
Marilyn Monroe died

Today they are worth
being baptized in the Jordan River

Tonight they will be worth
a dance with a pretty girl
and
maybe getting laid

Time Machine, 1942
Meri Harary

Cleaning woman,
calloused hands cradling a mop,
ammonia filling your lungs every day
since arriving in America,
behind the curtain, you stare
from your second floor tenement window,
yellow taxi curbed on Lincoln Place.
You smell the fumes from the engine
growling like an angry man.
Taxi's seats, soft like a casket,
will encase you and your unborn baby
if you ride to the clinic
to remove this third child,
the one you cannot afford—
you will be her tomb.

You do not know it is a girl;
eyes closed, curled within you
like your family in Germany
who could no longer remain hidden
in their Berlin flat—
packed into a dark train, no windows,
no night or day, no more time:
your baby sleeps concealed
in the blanket of your womb–
waiting to be cherished
or dissected and discarded.

You must decide to walk
down the narrow hallway,
through the steel door
with the peeling green paint
into the taxi, idling,
carbon monoxide smoke
rising from its tail pipe.
like the smoke from crematory chimneys.

Peering inside the taxi,
you see empty seats,
but we are there,
future generations within you,
like seeds not yet planted,
waiting to vanish
or be brought to life.

I'm From
Markita Hawkins

I'm from the struggle and havin' to snuggle up cuz we neva had any heat let alone socks or shoes or clothes on our backs, neva havin' any food in the fridgerator to eat at all because momma getting high off of what's upon the streets, disappearing for days, maybe even weeks. I'm from foster home to foster home, group homes and shelters. I'm from people sayin' no one can help her. They not talkin' about her, they talkin' about me. Yeah, I know it's every man for himself in this struggling society. Bad, yeah. Look, it's the economy. Government, don't lie to me, don't lie to us cuz I could have sworn the dollar bill said "In God we trust." And look at us saying we must have this, we must have that and ain't got ish to sho or ish to match. I'm from bogus relationships, tricks, offs and money. I look back on it now and think it's funny. I'm from a father that don't know me or care what I'm destined to be, but it's all good cuz he ain't is to me. I'm from trying to be strong and erase the weak, but it gets too late. I start to feel my eyes leak. I start to breathe heavy just thinking about the people that left and so-called loved me. I'm from being so blinded, so blinded that I can see what life has in store especially for me. I'm from gospel, art, hip-hop, R&B to express my feelings through songs and poetry.

Dream of Rebirth
Roberta Hill

We stand at the edge of wounds, hugging canned meat,
waiting for owls to come grind
night-smell in our ears. Over fields,
darkness has been rumbling. Crows gather.
Our luxuries are hatred. Grief. Worn-out hands
carry the pale remains of forgotten murders.
If I could only lull or change this slow hunger,
this midnight swollen four hundred years.

Groping within us are cries yet unheard.
We are born with cobwebs in our mouths
bleeding prophecies.
Yet within this interior, a spirit kindles
moonlight glittering deep into the sea.
These seeds take root in the hush
of dusk. Songs a thin echo, heal the salted marsh,
and yield visions untrembling in our grip.

I dreamed an absolute silence birds had fled.
The sun, a meager hope, again was sacred.
We need to be purified by fury.
Once more eagles will restore our prayers.
We'll forget the strangeness of your pity.
Some will anoint the graves with pollen.
Some of us may wake unashamed.
Some will rise that clear morning like the swallows.

Grieving Grandfather
Tanya Hough

He stood there
Tall, unavoidable, loud
His voice cracking
Tears streaming down his face

He is pleading
Trying to be heard
He is reaching out
Crying for help

Stop the violence
Stop the violence

His granddaughter was killed
Another child is taken
Another life is claimed
He stands before our eyes
He is pleading for money
to purchase flowers for the funeral that day

Stop the violence
Stop the violence

We are uncomfortable
Poverty stands before us
A face

A voice
A story

Stop the violence
Stop the violence.

We avoid eye contact
Too painful
Suffering, grief, pain
We don't want to relate.

Stop the violence
Stop the violence

He stands before us

Displaying a picture of his granddaughter
Innocence is lost
Fear is present
We can't look
WE can't look

Stop the violence
Stop the violence

His message is clear
Before us he stands
Tall, crying, pleading
Ever-present
Unafraid
He will be heard

Stop the violence
Stop the violence

We sit silently
Looking away
Pretending we can't hear his cries
To acknowledge is to relate
To relate is to feel
To feel is to connect
To connect is to realize we are the same
A face
A voice
A story

Food Drive
Scott Hutchison

Mrs. Bishop *knows*. When Jordan brought in
a case of canned hams, parading under the load
in front of the class, dumping them in the collection box
so hard they dented—applause from the desks, him bowing
at the waist and money-smiling—Mrs. Bishop came over,
put her hand on my shoulder and smiled down.

She held me back at recess, handed me a can
of Vienna sausage and some Ramen noodles to put in my backpack
till I felt comfortable to take my turn going forward to the box
and making my contribution. Nice lady. Last night
Mama put her hand over her forehead and rubbed
at the worry furrowing into her brain, served up "sandwiches"

of peanut butter and jelly between saltines. They're
my favorite. I always tell her so. And I was able to add
a Red Delicious apple from my lunch for us to split.
Yesterday at recess Jordan told everybody I was a free-luncher,
and the boys got me out of sight behind the big oak
playing the "free-puncher" game with me. I don't tell.

Talking about it makes it worse. All I know is, today when
the room re-filled and the bluster died down, Mrs. Bishop
arched her eyebrows my way. I shook my head
and gnawed on my pencil. All I know is, Mama
will be so surprised tonight to come home and see I've contributed,
I've made the meal, *me*—sausage and noodles—just for her.

Karachi's Centripetal Force
Zehra Imam

Flooded are the jagged streets after rain.
Flower sellers, clutching colors unsought,
Splash to cleanse the soles of their feet, in vain,
The business of beggars is at a halt.
College classrooms, too, with vacant seats lie.
Fruit vendors, with little chance to gain
any extra profit, swat away greedy flies.
Sewer water, rain water: Sewer-Rain…
Across the bridge where houses get bigger
samosas are served with steaming sweet tea
"Romance is the mood the monsoon triggers,"
says a lady with refined-looking feet
wrapped around in a sari of royal blue;
Sewer-rain shades brown the city's gray hues.

From Dovetailed Corners
Jim Johnson

There was a strip of color between this world and the next. Sulo
saw it in the east in the morning when he went to work and they
lowered him in the cage into the earth. He saw it in the west when he rose
again from the dead. Martha saw it too. Even when she was so
old she had forgotten so long into her past she could only remember
what was the beginning was the earth curving slowly into gray,
except for that thin streak between what was and what will be. That
she wove into her rugs.

***

Now in Northeastern Minnesota the mines shut down. Around
here it is said the unemployed outnumber even the mosquitoes. They
leave their eggs in snowmelt marshes, water-filled tree hollows,
hoof prints, or the tracks of logging trucks. Their eggs lying dormant,
overwinter, then when thawed come to life. The pupa breathing
through trumpets splits out of its skin into a winged adult. The
female is attracted by warm moist blood, needing blood for eggs.
Needing blood for eggs.

On Reading the Rocking Horse Winner

Lisa Kang

> And so the house came to be haunted by
> the unspoken phrase: *There must be more
> money! There must be more money!* The
> children could hear it all the time, though
> nobody spoke it aloud.
> —D. H. Lawrence

And I hear that whisper
In our house, too.
In the phone's incessant
Wail, stacked envelopes,
Door knocks, debates:
What should we pay first?
The hospital? The house?
Where can we go? And tiny
Hands offer hoarded treasures:
I have $7.32 can we stay?
And the children ask,
When Dad is well
And you finish your degree,
Then start to teach full-time
With benefits, will you smile
again sometimes? Will you
Sit with me and watch movies
Like you did before? And I study
And I type and I wait at the mailbox

For inevitable rejections. I search
And apply and interview and work,
Ten hours here, twelve hours there,
And above all I want to know: am I
The valiant rocking-horse winner
Striving against the odds,
Or his hateful mother
Who can never have enough?

Uncle Dolan Spoke on Timbering in East Tennessee

Kathryn Kerr

We cut six days, twelve hours,
waist deep snow in winter,
a hundred degrees in summer,
sharpened our axes and saws at night.

Streams stayed icy in summer,
froze in winter, not much
time for bathing. Wet clothes hung
in the room where we slept, fifty men.

Worst was the graybacks biting.
We scratched and cussed in sleep.
Kerosene would get rid of them
but it wouldn't keep them away.

But grub was plenty,
steak and eggs for breakfast,
biscuits, beans and ham, potatoes.
It was better than mining.

I
After Achieving
the American Dream

Susan Deborah King

My brother and I, ten and thirteen,
through the kitchen window
of our U-shaped house
through sheer curtains
of the lit bedroom
across the darkened courtyard
next to the pool
saw my father bring his fist
down and down upon our mother.
She cringed. We heard her yelp.
He kept at it, until he stormed out
flinging curses in his wake, calling me,
who'd always been his favorite,
You little bitch! Where was he going?
Why? Would he ever come back?
It took years and years to know,
it wasn't us. It was his own demons
gone berserk from all that gin.
Ahead lay weeks of facing school
with no one to tell, our mother
whimpering all day in bed—
broken spirit, broken ribs,

cereal every meal, the loss of the house,
a cramped, rat-infested apartment,
bankruptcy, suicide—homicide…
They've all been gone a long, long while.
My brother tried to fight it into coming right
and went completely off the rails.
I fled into books and friends–into God,
not sure I've ever fully come back out.

II

The Dream Debunked

Why do we decide to strive *not*
for all beings to have: bound wounds,
a full bowl, a pillow, a roof,
strong bonds
one to the other and time
to appreciate the music wind
plays with leaves, but
for climbing to the heaptop
to be above
looking down on neighbors,
too far removed to hear,
theirs or they ours, the cries, the crying?

My Choice, Not to Ignore the Poor's Voice

Jonathan C. Langley

A big hallelujah!

For outreach missions on which the poor are depending

Where would they all be?

If not for that giving

Some of the less fortunate suffer

Because states raise taxes on grounds not owned

Our government approving this for reasons unknown

Millions of homes foreclosed from bad loans

With no preventative pity from state to state

Why is it that the weak can never catch a break?

Why are the not-wealthy not given breaks?

And always getting rescued when it's already too late?

Maybe the answer

Is due to former leaders' poor decisions

That have affected the minority

Those who seem to be hidden

Quilts are given out

In the mouth of Center City

From many genuine hearts

Maybe some out of pity

Nevertheless

At least they chose to give

Helping the forgotten

To better how they live

A hot plate of food

And a cold drink of juice
Can heal any parched throat
Lack of nourishment can make one choke
The library downtown
Across from where the destitute crawl
Near where the street and the sub tunnel
Has become their outdoor stall
To escape their harsh reality
Some may gulp down beers
Jobs have been lost at lightening rates
Sometimes you wonder if the world cares
Until your home is foreclosed on
Some people never face that fear
But when they face devastation of a home
Reality hits when homes disappear
The only thing we can all afford—it's free–
Is something we can feel and hear
And that, ladies and gentlemen,
Is something we call the air
The homeless
Here is their description.
The diseases some of them face
Require many prescriptions
The filth on their garments
The tears from their eyes
The holes in their sneakers
The sounds of their cries
As loud as a boom! From a speaker
And an echo from a mountain
Just who has the generosity?
To let them drink from their fountain?
At least they don't have to worry

About the bills and collections
They are the minority
Feeling unworthy to vote during election
They need wholesome love and affection
Many are ashamed to get treated for infection
Not because they don't want the treatment
Just ashamed of their dirty midsection
I been where they been
Due to my parents co-signing for my siblings
We lost our home due to bad interest dealings
That's when it all hit the ceiling
I was only 18-years-old
Fresh out of high school
But I realized that my mind
Was my hope and greatest tool
My pastor brought me clothes
And our friendship became closer
I cried, and like a father
He let my head rest on his shoulder
Funding seems hard to come by
For human beings that help the city
While funds are endless to rescue dogs
And other animals including kitties
The city is always busy
Especially near city hall
The same area that the homeless lay
Where millions of dollars are spent at malls
Minimum wage has been on a standstill
For a period that seems the longest
Just writing about it
Makes me nauseous
Why do I write this?

It is because I used to live this
Upon no one not even an enemy
Would I ever hope and wish this
My only escape is my gift to write
I hope it will bring others delight
And pay for my future house and bite
For now I must assist the poor in this fight
From this gift I have to write
I do have a place to live now
But others still sleep in the park at night
I'm just being transparent
I'm the voice of the forgotten

Wetback
Luis Larin

The wetback crossed the arid desert
without water, but with dreams.
Without breath, but with life.
Wet, but afraid of ICE.
The wetback searched for the road to return on,
without knowing where he had entered
with the same dream of one day seeing change in the world.
The wetback found himself thirsty for justice.

The color of racism burned the wetback
but it didn't kill him
The wetback felt broken
like one broken raindrop in summer.
The wetback is who writes.
That wetback is me.

Dragon Flame Tattoo
James Lenfestey

Dragon's breath roars up his forearm scars.
In the outside world, where the walls are inside,
such a beast never backs down, never cools.
Inside these walls of stone, his hands offer the first poem,
its broken heart writhing like dragon smoke.
Tonight as I gaze out the dark window,
something bright streaks across the sky—a young man
riding a dragon's broad back, breathing free.

A Dozen Reasons to Give Up Haggling Over the Price of Weavings

Roseann Lloyd

1   for the weaver herself who takes the bus to market at 4 AM

1.5 for the buck and half she brings home each day

2   for the discount rate *para dos* she offers too readily

3   for the 3 languages she speaks, working on the fourth

4   for her babies born after the war

        one for the cousin killed in the highlands

        one for the uncle in Minnesota

        two for the brother and sister hiding in Mexico

5   for the age she started to weave

6   for her favorite colors: canario, rojo, verde, morado, indigo y café

7   for the quetzal/dollar exchange

8   for the animals who dance in her cloth

        cat, quetzal, monarch, hummingbird, deer,

        squirrel eating chamomile, chick, dove

9   for the tortillas in her apron pocket

10 for the ten fingers she says she's lucky to have

11 for the family she has to feed

12 for the men, the dozens of unmarked graves

Looking at a Photograph of My Mother, Age 3

George Ella Lyon

Little one
in the hand-worked dress
let me lift you
from the porch where you sit
with two brothers and a hound
while your father
the new baby in his arms
stands proud
at the gate.
Inside, your mother
beats biscuits, takes
a saucer edge to meat.

Hard times
line your daddy's hands
with sawdust, hone
your mother's wits
and her tongue.
Seven children
quick as flesh can bear them.
Even deep sleep
cracks with mouths.

Axe and saw
log hook and level

your daddy shaves hills
for your bread.
Your mother packs up
kettle and quilts
and piano when the sawmill
moves.

Crowded
at the foot
of some mountain
stashed at the head
of some creek
let me lift you.
You can look
like my son
over my shoulder
I will hold you.
Tell me
what you see.

1/
Chosen Lyric

I just need a lot of purpose
standing in these streets for years
& don't want to feel worthless
In QU they die from gunshots
in Suffolk the drugs make one stop
breathing
so many wakes and hearts bleeding
& people so sore they can't soar like eagles
and some doing time for illegal
I just wanna be the guy
that makes it
so a child wishes, staring at the sky
and says, If he can, why can't I?
& years later his mom & sis
tell poverty, "goodbye"
rappers freestyle, talk about their gun
but I don't, & they still say,
Lyric, you are the one
darkness and the streets
and u are the sun
Morton, I don't want to be the boss
please just get me where we need to be
& tell me the cost

Pastor Visits Parishioner
Marsha Matthews

I see them sitting on the couch, Almajean's hand held
by a man I don't know.

> His fingers feel every knuckle,
> every nail.

My eyes move to the ceiling, the plastic light bowl
frothed with wing dust.
Along the base,
an almost imperceptible crack.

> "This here's my cousin, Jeffrey, of Saltville,
> up far side of Clinch Mountain."

The hand he holds isn't hers.
Or is it? It isn't
attached.

> She looks at me looking,
> chuckles. "Oh you didn't know?
> Well, how could you?
> In church I clap right along with the rest."

> Jeffrey hands her the prosthesis.
> "See y-y-years ago,
> power saw slipped."

"Never mind." Amajean takes the hand
"I don't feel it."
She adjusts the pillow, leans back.
"The pain was someplace else."

She nods at the chair

I pull it close.

"Times was hard, then. Railroad on strike,
        my son—"
Her voice teeters.
        "was licking crumbs
        from cereal boxes
        thrown for trash.

        Talk about pain."

She attaches her hand.

        "If not for the insurance…"

                Jeffrey's eyes skirt my face,
my eyes on framed photos: her son,
Navy Seal, college graduate,
his eyes

        on Mom
        waving.

A Little Bit of Timely Advice
Mekeel McBride

Time you put on blue
shoes, high-heeled, sequined,
took yourself out dancing.

You been spending too much
time crying salty
dead-fish lakes into soup spoons,

holding look-alike contests
with doom. Baby, you
need to be moving. Ruin

ruins itself, no use unplanting
what's left of your garden.
Crank up the old radio

into lion-looking-for-food
music; or harmonica, all indigo,
breathing up sunrise. Down

and out's just another opinion
on up and over. You say
you got no makings

for a song? Sing anyway.
Best music's the stuff comes
rising out of nothing.

Deluge
Anne McCrady

In the heart-stopping darkness
of a clear day blindfolded
by the roiling, steely clouds
of not-enough-for-too-many,
a shared grief grips us.
Soaked with the rain of tears,
we huddle, sheltering children.
Done in by the dull cadence
of insult added to injury,
like the drip, drip, drip
of cold, soaked gutters,
we trudge through days
of sad and senseless stories:
one then another just like it
and another and another.
What began as a harmless
click-and-trickle of inequity
has swollen into a torrent,
until now there is no dry ground
for those who hunger for relief.
While the comfortable call
for action by nameless others,
stepping out of collective anguish,
a few brave souls open
umbrellas of practical prayers
and, as the flood of crisis rises,
they step forward into the deluge
to do, to bring, to be, to dream.

Tuesday at the Outreach Office
Ethna McKiernan

"Te amo hijo mio" Victor tells the child,
a two-year-old whose mother has run off.
They're here for help, for county benefits
they can't get without the child's birth certificate.
"No hablo espanol," I inform the dad
apologetically. Beyond a few stock phrases,
it's the truth. Victor has no English,
I have no Spanish, but the boy
now has a cup of applesauce
and so the dance begins—phone call
after phone call for referrals
to Spanish-speaking social workers,
and its 4:00 PM. I switch on
the speaker phone—finally, a lead,
and a volley of Spanish rains
into the conference room, her voice,
his voice, faster and faster. Victor slows,
hands the phone to me. The little boy
wants his mama, and we're missing one.
"It's complicated," the social worker says,
"the mother took the birth cert when she left,
the father lost his job because he had no one
to care for his son, they're behind $900 on the rent,
the eviction process has already begun,
the car's hanging on by a tire and a prayer,

and we can't even give him food stamps
without documentation. I'm referring him
to Legal Aid on Thursday." *"Si,"* I say,
"yes, *yo comprendo.*"
Victor lays his head down on the table
and weeps, a language we both understand.

After My Stepfather's Death
Wesley McNair

Again, it is the moment before I left home
for good, and my mother is sitting quietly
in the front seat while my stepfather pulls me
and my suitcase out of the car and begins
hurling my clothes, though now
I notice for the first time how the wind
unfolds my white shirt and puts its slow
arm in the sleeve of my blue shirt and lifts them
all into the air above our heads so beautifully
I want to shout at him to stop and look up
at what he has made, but when I turn
to him, a small man, bitter even this young
that the world will not go his way, my stepfather
still moves in his terrible anger, closing the trunk,
and closing himself into the car as hard as he can,
and speeding away into the last years of his life.

Mother and Child
Stephen Mead

Wheels & tracks, baby
Don't worry, I ain't gonna
Let you be taken. Hush-a-bye.
Hush-a-bye. Sleep now, that's right.
I got a couple hundred dollars
& in this knapsack you're pretty
Much hid just in case, you know,
That welfare lady's put out some
Warrant. O. K.
We're hitching a ride & will hop
The next train soon. 3 AM.
I think it's early enough,
The whole station still groggy.
Thank god, it's rainin', good
Warm muggy dust of diesel…
Makes me wanna doze too.
Come on, hon, don't wake up.
Here's your old tick tock clock,
Just like a heart, & I'm right
With ya, rockin' soft & close.
La la la. You see, I have to
Sing quiet, 'cause they're takin'
Our ticket and & hey, lettin' us board.
Nobody suspects. Want your bottle?
Look at those lights, the whole

City a Christmas tree blinkin'
"so long" as we plunge,
Express cargo, into the
Clickety-clack clickety-clack
Of this safe moving dark

Polenta
Marsha Mentzer

If I had known about polenta
when my laid-off father
returned with government surplus
brown bags of corn meal.

Tiny bowls of steaming corn meal mush,
cooled by splashes of milk
and sweetened with sprinkles of sugar,
for breakfast.

And sliced rectangles of hardened mush,
fried, crusty brown edges, hot,
drizzled with syrup,
for supper.

Who knew that mush was the perfect side,
served on hand-painted earthenware
at small corner bistros?

If only I had known that the
community center handout
was really polenta,
I would have eaten it
with delight, not shame.

Dedicated to the Countless South Africans Who Gave their Lives for Freedom and Democracy

Afzal Moola

Remember us when you pass this way.
we who fell,
who bled.
Remember us when you pass this way,
we who fell so that countless others may stand,
we who bore the brunt of the oppressor's hand.

Remember us when you pass this way.
Leave a flower or two as you pass along.
Sing! Sing for us a joyous and spirited song.

Remember us when you pass this way,
we who fell,
who bled.
Remember us when you pass this way.

Remember us in your tomorrows
as you remember us today.

Depression Generation
Sharon Lack Munson

Mother saved her weekly allotment
in heavy brown envelopes
taken from my father's store–
each pouch titled in her large flowing hand
Egg Lady, Dry Cleaners, Milkman.

She was ready when women from outlying farms
knocked on the side door
to deliver warm brown eggs,
or when the milkman brought
cheese, butter, cream.

She was prepared to pay the newsboy
for the daily Free Press,
Mr. Grossberg's delivery van
for freshly-baked seeded hard rolls.
I watched Mother budget her pennies.

Decades later I will clean out her apartment,
bring down from upper shelves
one rose-colored lace nightgown wrapped in tissue
still in its gift box,
slips too lovely and fragile for everyday wear.
In her bottom dresser drawer, I discover
nylons, still packaged, in the sheerest of shades,
black elbow-length gloves, just in case.

I kneel on the worn yellowed carpet,
crush delicate fabric tween my fingers,
bury my face, breathe smells of talcum
mixed with the fragrance of Coty's L'Origan.
I rock back. The familiar room encircles.

They're Coming to Take Us Away

Sharon Nelms

Hey, Hey!
please leave my typewriter
and my used computer
I saved for years
to buy

my eight-year-old Buick
my exercise bike
my thirty-year-old furniture
left over from a divorce ten years ago

I don't make enough
money to replace
anything

how will I ever
survive if the IRS
does what
they

threatened to do

maybe suicide
or cancer
is my
answer

who cares if they come

Washboard Wizard Highland, Kansas 1888

Marilyn Nelson

All of us took our clothes to Carver.
He is a wizard with a wash board,
a genie of elbow grease and suds.
We'll take you over there next week;
by that time you'll be needing him.
He's a colored boy, a few years older
than we are, real smart. But he stays
in his place. They say
he was offered a scholarship
to the college. I don't know
what happened, but they say
that's why he's here in town.
Lives alone, in a little shack
filled with books
over on Poverty Row.
They say he reads them.
Dried plants, rocks, jars of colors.
A bubbling cauldron of laundry.
Pictures of flowers and landscapes.
They say he painted them.
They say he was turned away when he got here,
because he's a nigger. I don't know about
all that. But he's the best
wash woman in town.

Head Start Kids
Kara Newhouse

These children are not my charity.
They are not some Other,
poor with names I can't pronounce
They are my neighbors' kids
chasing each other through the alley when the weather turns warm
They are the next set of teens
cracking jokes outside the Laundromat where I wash my clothes
These children are not my charity.
I walk home among the same trash piles and bombed-out buildings
as their size-three feet tread toting Superman backpacks
These children are not my charity
They need food, shelter, love and a good education.
These children are not my charity.
These children are just like me.

Why Shouldn't She

Grace Nichols

My mother loved cooking
but hated washing up
Why shouldn't she?
      cooking was an art
she could move her lips to
then the pleasure
feeding the proverbial
multitude (us)
on less than a loaf
and two fishes

Real Estate
Naomi Shihab Nye

Daddy picked up pamphlets at every stop
He was looking for another home, a place
to get away to. If you lose
your first home you loved so much,
you may be doomed. He bought
fifty acres, mouse-ridden house,
shabby barn. And kept looking.

My friend said when she was dying,
"We have to put on our armor of joy."
Maybe putting on another house
meant happy marriage, strong heart.
If he had another master bedroom, he might
become a master.

Figure out what you're searching for, cul-de-sac
mature trees, sprinkler system, wooden deck
totally renovated spacious floor plan
fantastic location, gleaming hardwood floors
executive style, dramatic hilltop view.

Even in the last months when all the blood
from the sweet haven of his olive-skinned body
cycled through a filtering machine every two days
he was thinking hilltop view—could he see all the way
across the ocean from there, the wrought-iron staircase,
the red-tiled roof?

Entitlements
by Molly O'Dell

He gets his way. Coon dogs and a four wheel

drive truck. Smoking a cigarette, me beneath

him. Screaming. He likes to burn my skin

with the glowing butt. First time I see

a doctor she counts the scars. Asks

why I stay. I come home thinking. He reads

my mind, says I'm so dumb the social worker

would take the baby. He makes twenty dollars

an hour. I make none back in the mountain.

This time I come to the doctor for a cut

on my head. Two for real, but one's covered

when I pull my hair back. He drove our sledge

hammer into my skull. Baby's seven, saw her

daddy do it. He's in jail now. I've got

MedRide. I'm making plans to get my way.

The Beloved Is Dead

Gregory Orr

The beloved is dead. Limbs
And all the body's
Miraculous parts
Scattered across Egypt,
Stained with dark mud.

We must find them, gather
Them together, bring them
Into a single place
As an anthologist might collect
All the poems that matter
Into a single book, a book
Which is the body of the beloved,
Which is the world.

Posture
Maureen Owen

When you're down and under and crushed and shattered
smashed and trodden and beaten, bamboozled, kicked and
destroyed lost out, gone mad, fell back, shot up,
done in, wiped out When your heart is broken and
your nose is running, your days are numbered, your lot
is cast, you're wasted, worried, choked up and ruined
left out, disinherited, sweating, frustrated, alone and
demolished, hopeless, despairing, depressed and insane
you're lousy you know it you wish you could change
Your coat's ripped, your nose is crooked, your brain
is mush, your hands are cursed, your life is worthless
and you're uncomfortable a hunchback, a sucker,
a recluse, a frog When you know you can't make it
You're hideous, helpless, pusillanimous, squirrelly and
dumb

> just bear in mind
> that 9/10s of everything
> is posture

> Stand up!

Don't Close Larry's
Carl Palmer

Larry's Payday Loans out on the avenue
don't ask if I even have a payday
which I do most of the time
but there're times when I don't
there's once or twice been occasion
even with a payday I had to hit Larry's
maybe not enough hours or missed a day
don't get paid when Cecilia's sick
be different if she had a momma home
to be there with her while I work

Larry's may charge something extra
but I'm good for it I got my pride
I don't need but a bit to get me by
don't have to sit and wait no interview
explain why and what for
no embarrassment having to ask
humiliation by being turned down
don't want my daughter's daddy on welfare
any day now I'll break out of this loop
hand to mouth payday to payday

I don't go by Larry's Loans every week
seen folk that do—vicious cycle
Getting deeper desperate destitute

but then the rich do the same thing
credit cards boats clothes fancy cars
some roadside loan outfits are predators
so are store cards zero down no interest
no fees for a year everyone qualifies
Larry's is just Larry's good for folks like me
let him be he needs to make a living too.

The Hyperbolist Speaks
Pit Menousek Pinegar

One daughter calls me a hyperbolist,
the other says she has cast herself
in my Drama Queen mold—I'd swear
it was the other way around:
my drama reaching out to meet
her drama head-on. My son says
I exaggerate, that my humor
is iffy; really, I'm trying
my damnedest to be a good sport.
I want them to notice who and what
I am without having to shout, "Woe is me!"
or " Bring on the hearse!" or "…the rack!"
or "…the straight jacket." I want to
bring out some compassion in them
without drawing attention to the fact
that I've become the poster woman
for economic disaster, one of those
who started out securely enough,
has fallen, fallen again—and further.

Best I can tell, my children are all content
with what they can afford. Only one owns
property, two drive cars, none have children.

I'm sure they think of me as old—how could
they not? They're in early middle age—
too young for crises—and I was nearly thirty
when the eldest was born.

It is July, a hundred degrees. I stumble across
the hilly campus where I teach summers. I'm not
sure I can't walk one more football field length
in the blistering sun without falling. I cry
in the car before the air conditioning kicks in—
not a whit of hyperbole there.

I send a joint text to the kids: "I am hot,
hot, hot," it says, "perhaps I'm dying." Maybe
I'll get a laugh, a little sympathy. One says,
"It's rude to multi-text your children
or anyone else." (*They* have phones with
proper keyboards; mine's a 10-year-old
Razor: *Hit once for a, twice for b, thrice
for c, hit four times for 2.*) The second says,
"You exaggerate." The third doesn't respond.
"You can say a mass in my name," I say.
(We're not Catholic.) "Give me a break!" says one.
"Sit Shiva," I say, "say Kaddish." (We're not Jewish,
either, though both my oldest cousin and I
always suspected it was the part of the story
our fathers left out.) "Oh, for crying out loud,"
says the second. "Yes, that would be fine,"
I say, "feel free to wail on my behalf."
The eldest remains provocatively silent.

Since I can stir no sympathy, I have no
choice but to feel a wee bit sorry for myself.
I've already worked more than ten years longer
than all those male doctors, bankers, professors,
and chiefs in my family. I'm the one economists
are talking about when they talk about the down-

wardly mobile descent from one economic class
to another, the one who has fallen through
cracks, fallen into shabbiness and disrepair,
whose angst about energy resources is not
world-view-green, but platelet-red and fading
to world-class anemia not worth stanching.

"I'm bleeding money," I say. "For Godssake
Mom," —the oldest finally checks in—
"you've been to third world countries,
you've been in the north or south ends
of a dozen cities in this country; you know
what poverty is." "My car is old enough to
collect social security," I reply. "I don't have
a car," she says, "I ride a bike to work."

I live in a house I can no longer afford.
I drive a car that is just short of *vintage*.
"Thanks, old car," I say; I pat the dash,
each time the engine turns over, each time
the car rolls uneventfully into the drive.
"Good ride," I say out loud, "I appreciate
your excellent service." My daughter,
the one who calls me a hyperbolist,
says I am not grateful for what I have.
She does not hear me talk to my car;
she does not bear witness to
my daily incantations of prayer-like gratitude:
for my heart's steady beat, for the roof
that doesn't leak, for the generosity of friends,
for work that turns time timeless, for other work
that's rarely boring, for having once had

the Biggest Love imaginable—though
not everlasting—for the privilege of children,
for sufficient curiosity, strength, endurance
to get me this far. Still, I have a dozen deep
wounds at being without so much I once thought
basic and essential. I try very hard for that
third-world view my daughter thinks I should
have. I try not to think of all that's been taken,
to appreciate instead trees, clean water,
bluest skies, rain after a sweltering day,
old clothes that aren't rags, a continuing,
if sometimes marginal, sense of humor
which abandons me altogether
from time to time, and then I think this:

I have borne and raised three, minimalist,
childless children who are careful to live
within their means. They're not exactly smug,
just clear, matter-of-fact. They do not recall
when I bought new cars for cash saved hard—
though two were mid-teens the first time
I bought a car on time—had one credit card
cleared every thirty days, no mortgage,
no home equity line of credit.
I was a marker for fiscal responsibility,
economic restraint. With any luck
they won't connect the dots and know
that in the end, it was the three of them
I couldn't afford—a fact single mothers
work hard to keep from their children.

To Hope
Martha Postlethwaite

Doesn't mean you have reason to believe you will get what you want.
Doesn't mean the disease will be cured,
      or your lover will come back.
Doesn't mean that all who suffer cruelty will be saved.
Doesn't mean that after you die you will go to Heaven.
Doesn't even mean you will be able to forgive yourself.

Hope is immediate.
It is the mind that can pause to notice
      the deep intake of breath,

                followed by the slow exhale.
Hope is your lungs rejoicing
      and your heart
drumming   to   beat   the   band.
Hope is your body,
      composting food the earth has spent herself to give you,
          to fuel the day.
Hope is the miracle of waking
      and with any luck,
          remembering a dream

The Unchosen
David Radavich

We are the unselect,
those not favored

by any god
among the victors.

We are not asked
to join a team,

we lose so
others may lord it,

our soil is stolen
without acknowledgment

so those expanding
can feel gain.

Our food
tastes of leavings,

our blood circulates
in dry channels.

Sun shining
on us is not golden

but a kind of glare
seeing grief.

Even at night
sleep is fitful, a mouse

is stealing the last morsel
and the moon eats

itself thin

with plans for
the full awakening.

Blood: Whose and How Much
Carlos Reyes

At the hide factory the men lounge
atop piles of fresh and bloody skins
puff tailor-made cigarettes and choke
down sandwiches of cheese and bologna

Across town in the poultry plant
in rubber boots Alice, in four inches
of blood and water, stands waiting
for the next bird hanging
to come around on the conveyor

The odor of offal drives off

her craving for food, even if
she's hungry, the conveyor
never stops for lunch–she waits
for another throat to slit, waits
for it to bleed out the few dollars

her daily bread.

My Vision Has Rhythm
Lola Rodriguez

My vision has rhythm,
The lyric of eloquent buds
Popping on loud branches,
The uproar of flowers forming.

The pulse of the moon
In its track,
An oscillating beam
Thundering
A silver wash through shadows;
The deep bass of night.

My vision has rhythm,
The music of moist heat
Rising from the solid beat
Of sidewalks
In the yellow day.
The small crash of poverty,
Its trumpet-blast
Of silence.
The bitter thump
Of love
And the swell of the river.
The tender boom of faith,
The clamor of fortune.

My vision has rhythm,
Its uproar
Clatters in the air
Pounds the earth
The eyes, dance together.
The heart rolls, a drum.

Justification of the Horned Lizard
Pattiann Rogers

I don't know why the horned lizard wants to live.
It's so ugly–short prickly horns and scowling
Eyes, lipless smile forced forever by bone,
Hideous scaly hollow where its nose should be.

I don't know what the horned lizard has to live for,
Skittering over the sun-irritated sand, scraping
The hot dusty brambles. It never sees anything but gravel
Creosote bush, the ocotillo and its whiplike
Branches, the severe edges of the Spanish dagger.
Even shade is either barren rock or barb.

The horned lizard will never know
A lush thing in its life. It will never see the flower
Of the water-filled lobelia bent over a clear
Shallow creek. It will never know moss floating
In waves in the current by the bank or the blue-blown
Fronds of the water clover. It will never have a smooth
Glistening belly of white like the bullfrog or a dewy-heavy
Trill like the mating toad. It will never slip easily
Through mud like the skink or squat in the dank humus
at the bottom of a decaying forest in daytime.
It will never be free of dust. The only drink it will ever know
Is in the body of a bug.

And the horned lizard possesses nothing noble—
Embarrassing tail, warty hide covered with sharp dirty

Scales. No touch to its body, even from its own kind,
Could ever be delicate or caressing.

I don't know why the horned lizard wants to live.
Yet threatened, it burrows frantically into the sand
With a surprisingly determined fury of forehead, limbs
And ribs. Pursued, it even fights for itself, almost rising up,
Posturing on its bowed legs, propelling blood out of its eyes
In tight straight streams shot directly at the source
Of its possible extinction. It fights for itself,
Almost rising up, as if the performance of that act,
The posture, the propulsion of the blood itself,
Were justification enough and the only reason needed.

Free-wheeling Through Meffa
Abigail Rome

Decades ago and just out of college, I tried out life in the city.
Crowded, rutted streets and decades-old houses with grey metal siding
And green and white striped awnings with scalloped edges.
A place where people labored and argued as their way of life.
Their only pleasure, a pick-up baseball game with bases made of balled up tee shirts.

I had grown up among expansive grassy lawns, houses spaced adequately apart.
We all went to summer camp and most attended Ivy League schools.
At my college, perched on a quiet hill, perfect in its symmetry of brick halls,
I studied biology with a plan to save the rainforests.
Or, if not that, to study life in the intertidal zone.

Foreign to me were Italian mothers yelling at their children all hours of the day,
Irish grandparents rocking aimlessly on their front stoops.
Too many white plaster Mother Marys on half-shells,
Speaking of family history, blind faith, and centuries of oppression.
Not my cup of tea. I needed reprieve.

There was no Spandex then. My shoes had no cleats, my pedals no clips.
I just jumped aboard, letting one thigh push, and then the other.
Round and round, I gained momentum. The world moved by faster and faster,
Blurring those kitchy-facaded houses with their plastic flowers in window boxes,
The city's neighborhoods melding into a richly-textured work of art.

The Adventure
Helen Klein Ross

A shampooist in an uptown hair salon warns a matron not to lean too far
back on the sink.
The salon is being renovated and
                    the sink needs adjustment.

The shampooist is new. This time last year, she wasn't a shampooist, she
was a chemist.
                    in a country now erased by a war.

This is an adventure, the matron observes gingerly tilting her head back
until it rests on
                    the porcelain.

Yes, an adventure, the shampooist says, reaching for a towel to cushion
her neck.

My Name
Rose Schwab

My name has long white hair.
My name wears overalls and grew up on the Kansas prairie.
My name has floated down rivers
     that turned around and puzzled over their wandering path
     and then smiled mischievously and set their teeth.
My name is complicated, and tall, with icy blue eyes.
My name cooks in its nicest dress shirt
     to prove how clean it can be.
My name has a mind for mathematics
     and a red beard.
My name says that no matter what happens,
     we will go through it together.

Brother Sighting

Karen Seay

That summer day
I was driving north on 169 during rush hour.
At the bridge over the intersection with Minnetonka Blvd.
I looked down the ramp where cars are backed up at the light,
and saw him there.

> I thought he was such a miracle
> > the day we brought him home from the hospital
> > > wrapped in that blue blanket.

His long gray braid hung down his back;
he was holding his sign,
and the old bright pink bicycle I gave him when I got a new one
was lying next to him on the ground.

A few seconds later I crossed the railroad bridge
and passed over what had been his home for several summers,
until the police decided it wasn't any more.

The Snow Cave Woman

Anne E. Seltz

One night she slept in a snow cave
    A cave she dug in the pile of snow
    On our church lawn
    She had no other home

The police said—*Destroy it—It's not safe*
    We said, No
    We will honor this sacred space
    And we will scream to help her find a home
    Though we know her not

Oh Holy one, help us get out of our own cave
    Our cave of unawareness
    Our cave of comfort
    Our cave of isolation from that snow cave woman

"Escape" Artist

Gene Severson

Aunts and uncles
cousins and spouses
engaged in a maddening orgy
of small talk.
From every corner
of the house
muffled noises,
indistinct sounds,
yips and yells.
Enough already!

So I took my glove
and went out
and threw the ball
against the house
over and over again
as I usually did
when I needed to escape.

"Stop that!"
everybody in the house
screamed.
You're making
too much noise!
I just kept tossing.

Pink Slip
Betsy Sholl

Twenty years I gripped your press,
yanked down as the belt rattled past.
You stamped my checks, the bank sent letters
saying what I owed on my house, my car,
my teeth. Now the expressway roars overhead,
and how can I argue back, when I can't

even get my car out of the tow lot?
Inside the gatekeeper's shed a TV surfs
out of control: soap commercial, canned laughter,
profile of Martin Luther King, skinny woman
stepping out of a fat woman's clothes—
as I would like to step out of this night

onto the last day of earth and accuse you
once again, only now with smoke and lights,
some kind of music to back me up:
how my kids are the same age as yours,
my kids with too many teeth in their heads,
and one who still can't pronounce thr—.

All you did was check your watch,
all you did was back me to the door,
where outside they were hauling my car,
a pirate company, so not even the cops
could say where it is. Is this America?
I've seen countries on TV where the natives

give funny looks to the fat men they serve
drinks to on patios. "Bastard," would be
my translation. Or whatever the deaf woman
is banging onto the locked windows of cars
jammed at the on-ramp trying to leave the city.
You on your top floor look down, waiting

for the crowd to thin, you with those women
in high heels printing out memos that shut
down a whole plant. You're calm now.
But if just one loony on the picket line
decides to fling a bucket of paint,
if a pack of kids with bats comes hooting out

of a bar, you wouldn't have a clue.
One more John Doe in fancy clothes,
high class words foaming on your lips,
but just as helpless, you bastard,
at the end of the world, if there is an end,
if people like me get to rise up and speak.

Slum Boy on Glue
Michael Shorb

between midnight
and the rough stones
walling off the world's
treasures thick bullet
proof glass and sparkling
Christmas angel away
you can't imagine how I feel
after the third inhalation
glitters its way toward
the surge and bustle
of my heart and lungs
ablaze like a river and
my starved brain
tropical aurora borealis
frees me, dancing
down these diamond-
paved streets saying
I'm the boy who sings
cabin boy and minstrel's
wonder slum boy
and wharf rat's rival
huddled in warm
red blankets behind
the alley dumpster
near the plaza of heroes

the one with puppy eyes
and veins of icy stone
ready for death or dawn
whichever wears
the brightest helmet.

First of the Month Kool-Aid
Marty Silverthorne

It's raining; prostitutes and pimps,
illegitimate babies and infected
mothers, puddle around the fire barrel.
Crack falls out of the sky and the big
white moon shields its face behind
a cloud when it rolls over the hood.
An empty syringe hangs from a junkie's
arm and the forecast in his eyes is stormy.
White probation officers roll through
the rain of poverty and pain looking
to lock up a brother, some mother's
baby boy whose snow-filled nose
has him pissing jail time. Three little
black girls jump rope, me under the porch stoop:
rain, rain go away, the mailman bring the check today.
Mama plans the first-of-the-month meal,
takes a taxi to Piggly Wiggly on the corner
of Dickinson and Hooker to swap food stamps
for macaroni and cheese, neck bones, gizzards,
2 for 1 Jesse Jones Hotdogs. Up and down
the WIC aisle, she shops to fill her bare cupboards.
Down King Drive neighbors are getting high
in a shot house where they sold their stamps
to keep the dope sickness off. October rain
gurgles in the gutter mixed with last night's

blood of baby-faced black boy trying to win
his rights to wear blue and red bandanas.
Sirens squall by; it's another day, another
rainy day in the projects, children's lips
red with first-of-the-month Kool-Aid.

Bountiful
Claudia Solotaroff

In my youngest years, the only money I saw in my grandparents' house was in a sugar bowl on a shelf over the stove, between the motley ball of saved string and the soup can filled with pencils. You could say we lived in poverty, certainly at subsistence, on a tiny farm. The house was old, the furniture old too, soft, worn, faded and comfortable. Grandma cooked on a wood-burning stove. I lived with them because my parents were busy making money. "Trying to make money." "Working hard and long to make money." If anyone asked what my parents did I would have answered, "They make money." I did not know how money was made—I just knew it was fun—Grandma would take down the sugar bowl sometimes so I could play with the coins, stacking, sorting, counting, spinning and flipping them.

I thought money was part of a game grownups played. Sometimes Grandpa would take a few coins from the sugar bowl and we would walk to town. If he wanted a piece of hardware, or grandma a paper of pins, we could go into a store and trade one or two of the coins for what we needed. The best trade was giving one small coin, a dime, getting in return a big slab of licorice, and also a larger coin, a nickel that, when we got home, I could place in the sugar bowl with a satisfying "clink." It seemed that we always won, prospered, and we would always have what we needed and more.

Later I saw paper money. People would pull into our driveway in their cars, and Grandma would bring out from the porch paper bags of corn, eggs, tomatoes, beans, sometimes a dead, featherless, headless chicken. And the people would give her pieces of paper. Limp little pieces of sickly green paper. It seemed a bad trade, the opposite of Grandpa's coin-into-licorice trick. We had all worked to plant and water and pick the produce, to feed the chickens, to gather the eggs. Certainly we had much more than we could ever eat, but still, all this for paper? Those papers seemed to disappear; they had no sugar bowl to live in. Grandma lived to old age, and when she died my father took from under her bed a box she had prepared for her funeral. There was a new dress and new underwear and a thousand of the pale green papers, tied with string in bundles.

When I was six, I was taken to live with my parents and go to school. In their home in town, a small apartment, efficient, with all the modern conveniences. money was discussed often, certainly daily. My father liked to make money and keep it but my mother was driven to shop, to get "nice things." There were arguments. My mother usually won, so we had sharp, hard-edged pristine furniture and my mother and I had perfect outfits for every occasion. My father still was able to put money in the bank, and review his accounts, audibly, nightly, and rail at the goddamned taxes. We had plenty of everything but never enough.

To this day, money confuses me.

Bar

Aaron Stauffer

During one of the hardest
summers of my life,
I grew to love a bar.
It was expensive,
only served Rolling Rock
and was hardly ever open
when I needed it to be.
But its overly-fried
and burnt food and watery beer
still got you drunk
enough to enjoy a sunset
over the Hudson in Manhattan.

What a Wake Up Call
Madreen Stevens

I'd wake up to her coming into my bedroom
naked and screaming, *Don't touch me!*
Stop! Go away! Leave me alone!
Call the Police, Madreen! Call the Police!
as he stood in the doorway, wang
swinging in the breeze, and I,
an 11-year-old child stood between them,
my mother crouching down
on the floor behind me.

I'd say, *Get out of here!*
Leave her alone! Go away!

And when I could, when it was safe to,
after he left, I'd shake my head and ask,
Why do you do this to yourself?
Why do you go back to him?
The Police weren't called.

They were going through a scene
played out too many times
with the same ending.
They went back to each other.
I always thought it was stupid
and dangerous.

He could beat the s____ out of me
and still get to my ma
if he really wanted to.
I was only 3' 3" tall.

God must have been protecting me
even then, thanks to grandma's prayers.

Ballad
Black folklore on Thomas Jefferson
Tony Stoneburner

Helpless himself,
He couldn't be he
Without black people
Helping him be.

He couldn't shave
With the hot water,
The soap, the razor;
Without a slave.

He couldn't dress
So neat & trim
Without the slaves
Assisting him.

Or put boots on feet
Without their pull.
He couldn't eat
Until he was full
Without their service.

Or feel complete
Until bedding, he traces

Soft curves he craves
To the softest crevice
(she performing her office).

He couldn't be healthy
Without their help.

He'd sit in the dark
Till they lit the candles.
He'd not go out
Till they opened the door.

He wouldn't be wealthy
If they didn't hide
The family silver
When the redcoats came
Under the floor.

He wouldn't be free
If they hadn't been bridling
and saddling the horse
On which to ride;
If they didn't bring
Out of the stable
Fleet mount on which
Deft slaves enable
Master to flee.
Skedaddling
Faster and faster
When redcoats came.

He wouldn't be he
But for the slaves
Whose prompt & decisive
Action saves—
Decisive action
To guarantee
Happiness, Life,
& Liberty.

Trouble, Fly
Susan Marie Swanson

Trouble, fly
out of our house.
We left the window
open for you.

Fly like smoke from a chimney.
Fly like the whistle from a train.
Fly far, far
away from my family,
mumbling in their sleep.

Trouble, fly.
Let our night
be a night of peace.

Ten Gallons of Tough
Tiffany Tate

I know what it's like
Having to carry that
5-gallon bucket full of tough
I'm a woman in a man's world
Set down your bucket
they'll walk all over you
Drinking their 12-pack of cool
They'll run you down with lies
You'll be pulling out your
hard-knock-life knife
Ain't no one gonna let you
set down your 5-gallon bucket of tough
'cept me
I can set down mine, too
when I'm with you
We can pull out a bottle of honesty
in the evening, but
Pour me another morning, dear,
Plenty of sugar
to take away the bad taste of poverty.
Light up a prayer cigarette
and breathe out acceptance
dancing in the light.
You and me, babes
We're 10 gallons of tough

The War Is Over
John Thiemeyer

The old man with no color in his face wandered loosely down Lombard saluting every dark window he passed. It was approaching midnight, less than a week till Thanksgiving. A week from Armistice Day. 11-11-11. 11th hour. 11th minute. 11th day or the 11th month. The war in Iraq is over.

The old man saluted his reflection.

Everybody who thought they knew him said he was no damn Marine. He was just crazy. Been drunk since before dirt. Been a familiar in St Johns forever, walking and checking, walking and checking, never letting a pay phone get past him. Wasn't a coin slot that was safe when he was around.

They wouldn't even allow him in the bars these days. I saw him once try to get in Brad's, and even THEY wouldn't let him in. NO neighborhood tavern to call home.

Man, that's sad.

That's really doing something, getting barred from Brad's for life!

But he didn't remember.

Next night I saw him get barred again, like nothing from the night before had registered at all. When he left from that door, and that same bald-headed fuck yelling at him, telling him no one wanted him around, he checked the coin slot at the payphone he'd just passed and crossed the street oblivious.

I've seen him walk across Lombard in rush hour. Just lost in his bubble. But this night there were no cars. Everyone, it seemed, had disappeared. Only a ghost like him was about. The Spirit of Thanksgiving. Old St. Bic, I called him. Don't ask me why. Maybe because his flame was out of fluid. Like his brain, it'd all leaked out.

And all he could come up with to do this Sunday night when he had the stage of Lombard all to himself was thump on some dark store windows, pound on locked doors and yell for someone whose name was unintelligible. Over and over till he came to the corner and turned. Disappeared.

God knows where he lived. When I'd asked him, he looked right through me. Like I was the ghost.

Scribe
Kim Tran

Without home, paper kept me warm. Its rough fibers
against my raw skin spoke
the language of marginality,
of survival.

In icy wind, the newsprint would fold over itself
again and again,
doubling chances
and strength.

In these embarrassingly prestigious halls I experience a new frost.

Naked anew, looking to my old friend.
I find paper when I am infirm
and pen when I am weak.

To write poetry about my poetry,
the way I love my community
an inherited tradition,
a method that began with papyrus.

I carry her with me,
that small child who
pressed daisies between the pages of a dictionary
trying to make sense of love,
and hate, of pedagogy and paper.

Self-employment, 1970
Natasha Trethewey

Who to be today? So many choices,
all that natural human hair piled high,
curled and flipped—style after style,
perched, each on its Styrofoam head.
Maybe an upsweep, or finger waves
with a ponytail. Not a day passes
that she goes unkempt—
Never know who might stop by—
now that she works at home
pacing the cutting table,
or pumping the stiff pedal
of the bought-on-time Singer.

Most days, she dresses for the weather,
relentless sun, white heat. The one tree
nearest her workroom, a mimosa,
its whimsy of pink puffs cut back
for a child's swing set. And now, grandchildren—
it's come to this—a frenzy of shouts,
the constant slap of an old screen door.
At least the radio still swings jazz
just above the noise, and

Ah, yes, the window unit–leaky at best.
Sometimes she just stands still, lets
ice water drip onto upturned wrists.
Up under that wig, her head
sweating, hot as an idea.

Street Wise
Connie Walle

No rocking chair.
No grandchildren begging for stories.
No tea from a china cup.

Shivering, she pulls her
tattered coat closer to her.

Leaning over the grate, trying
to glean a little of its warmth.

Pulling newspaper from her bag
she wraps her feet, setting in for the night.

Slipping into sleep, she pushes
memories of better times away
lets the numbness set in.

Gone
Beverly Welsh

Ev'rything's gone;
no cows, pigs, chickens or cats.
The dog's buried in the woods.
The radio's gone,
all the furniture too.
Tractor, plow, mower all gone;
the grain bin's empty,
the hay mow bare,
apple tree cut down;
father gone, mother away,
children grown and gone;
ev'rything's gone.

Lakeview Lounge

John Wessel-McCoy

Hillbilly bar in Uptown
Jukebox plays the guys-with-the-hats
Didi smiles behind the bar
And asks me where's princess
Beer & whiskey with my buddy Steve
Cigarettes from the gas station.

 Another one found dead at work
 The police have come and gone
 Hauled the body away
 We made the calls
 Filed the paperwork
 Nothing more can be done today.

Drink, smoke, talk, feed the jukebox
"I Still Miss Someone"
Remember Jack. Remember Anthony
"Streets of Bakersfield"
Remember Gabriel, remember Ed
Remember Mike, remember all the dead.

 Cancer, AIDS, hearts giving out
 Hard-drinking, 'heron' and crack
 Scarred by Vietnam, prison and psych ward
 No longer hustling, no longer running
 Lonesome and broken, poor and dead on the floor
 Ugly, wretched, merciful death.

Remember "Sarge" had them all fooled
Anthony sheltered orphaned kittens
Gabriel's angry mind was brilliant
Ed's scarecrow frame shook when he laughed
Mike could have been my uncle
Don't children of God deserve better than this?

"Swinging Doors," "There Stands the Glass"
In the end we slip out the door
With one shot of Wild Turkey to go
Procession to the brick wall
Alley ritual to remember the dead
Glass shatters and whiskey rains.

Little Tree
Daniel Williams

Poor children in school
white black and brown
children with no shoes
thin children no coats
torn clothing lunchtime
children with not much
to eat but for delicious
stories at Christmas—
9 years of age and I felt
sorry for everything
even my orange peel
to which I apologized
before abandoning it
in the trash
I made up a story of a
tiny disfigured pine tree
adopted by a poor
family with only their
affection for decorations—
no angels no elves yet
teacher loved it
I made figures out of
flannel of my lop-sided
tree its trashcan base
the mother and father
the brother and sister
their wretched dog

their wreck of a house
I went through all
the classrooms
telling my story
how a golden star
magically appeared
on the tree's tip
to brighten their lives—
my squirming
audiences all paid
rapt attention so young
yet they knew already
the brilliance of imagination
over poverty

Witness

Tony Voss Williams

Moses stepped onto Nicollet
Looking for some breath and a cigarette
5 am Minnesota winters get checked
He's about 5 minutes from a bitter end
But he gotta get it in
Look, he got the ambition
If he could just turn into a business man
He could get up out the city
And move to a better kinda promised land
For now it's that daily dose of rat race
Couple dollars cash made
Couple bills backdate
A couple subtle backaches
Walking near the cafe
He sees a thief start running out the back way
Police on a fast chase
Thought Moses was a robber from his black face
Saw him in a bad place
He had his headphones on him
So he didn't hear the cops yell stop
'Til they shot him

Who'll be a witness for my lord
Who'll be a witness for my lord
Who'll be a witness for my lord
Who'll be a witness for my lord

My soul is a witness
My soul is a witness
My soul is a witness
My soul is a witness for my lord

It don't matter if you're guilty
Long as they can sell you on a guilty plea
They lock you in a box in a facility
While they make a profit off of your misery
It would cost less to send a criminal to college
But that ain't got the same kind of profitability
CCA: buy the stock in quantity
It's a profit livin' constant in villainy
Practically a modern day slave trade
You can't survive on a minimum wage pay grade
So if you can't wait for a pay day
You gotta get paid in less safe ways
Sell a couple grams til they hit you with the mace spray
And once you've done time in a jail
Ain't nobody wanna hire you
Provide for your health
We all prisoners of the wealth
Whether you locked in a cell or you locked in yourself

Who'll be a witness for my lord
Who'll be a witness for my lord
Who'll be a witness for my lord
Who'll be a witness for my lord

Pharaohs always breathe easy
Whether in a crown or a three piece
Just take a look around and believe me

The poor shoved down while the rich getting greedy
Live and die in sin
Give a few percent of income
Forget about the sickness
And try to fix the symptom
It's lunacy
We work to give a home
To communities
And Wells Fargo take 'em with impunity
The poor get arrested
Bankers get immunity
The story of the pharisee
Living under usury
History repeats and the leaders make green
Like they picked strange fruit left hanging off they trees
Occupy dreams,
Never let 'em sell you on the leash
If it means a rebellion in the streets
None of us are free
While poverty's a business
Tell me who the hell is gonna be a witness

Who'll be a witness for my lord
Who'll be a witness for my lord
Who'll be a witness for my lord
Who'll be a witness for my lord

My soul is a witness
My soul is a witness
My soul is a witness
My soul is a witness for my lord

Desert Cenote
Keith Wilson

There is sadness among the stones
today, the rabbits are silent.

No wind. The heat bears down.
It has not rained for one year.

We have faith out here, desert
people, we wait, knowing with sureness

the swift cross of clouds, the blessings
of moisture (to deprive a man is to give

charms to him). I love this dry land
am caught even by blowing sand, reaches

of hot winds. I am not the desert
but its real name is not so far from mine.

Namesake

Laura Madeline Wiseman

She tells me she needs to stop drinking, to lose weight
and get a job cleaning condos lining the blue bay
and the white sand beaches. She says, it's the easiest money,

and lists the ways you tackle a room, fridge first
to see what's left: the unopened, bottled, canned.
As she drinks she says, *I'm not picky like some of them.*

If there was take-out, half a steak, I'd take it home
and eat it. It's not like people spit on their food
and save it for later. A territorial act. She knows

I still want to call her Big Laura, her nickname.
She asked to be called Little Laura, my nickname.
She won't answer when I accidentally slip.

Spokane Reservation School Teacher: Welpinit, Washington

Carolyne Wright

They used to have a dentist all day
Thursday. Now, you wait three months
to hitch to Spokane when the root's ache
breaks your stoicism down. Sharp operators
still cut Indians open at the B.I.A.
To live here, stay on automatic, keep
emergency systems on all night,
miss your lover only once a week.
When the book mobile wheels in, hide there,
read how missionaries staked conversion
claims on tribes, worried at each other
like tribe terriers over buffalo scraps.
Your school's an old God-trap of theirs,
earthed up now like a sod-sided council lodge.
Teenagers pass furtive peace pipes
through the fence at recess. If you weren't
the boss, brought from the outside like a Jesus book,
you'd join them. Instead, you skirt the rules.

Jairus's Daughter
Pam Wynn

It's my job. Each night I say, "Yes, there
is room" or "No, there's none," then close the shelter
door and turn the key. Tonight the sky,
a thin layer of blue tissue paper,
spreads out, empty of moon and stars.
A girl whisks past across the threshold with
her chin tucked down into her chest, further
than I think humanly possible. Eighteen,
nineteen, jaw clenched, lips tight, she chooses
a spot upon the floor farthest from the door.
Later, her hair, now brushed into long, even
strands, fans across the pillow. She sleeps on
wrapped in sheets with swirls of yellow
flowers. Tattooed on her left cheek a small
dusky rose, and on her upper arm
two writhing snakes who watch over her.
Her lids flutter—a small sick bird—
perhaps that dream in which a Savior takes
the girl's hand, says, *Awake child, get up,*
and everyone rushes into the room
rejoicing and gives her something to eat.

A Hindu Prayer
Anu Yadov

Ok, I'm praying, ok?

I'm sitting on the toilet and I'm praying.

Let's just get one thing straight.

I don't believe in you.

I don't believe in Krishna.

God.

But I'm praying because I don't know what else to do.

I'm just going to talk to you even though

I don't believe in you, ok?

What has happened to me?

I am living on the edge of existence.

My medicine,

food for my daughter,

rent,

electric bill,

car payment,

I have to choose between

these

things.

These are impossible choices.

I want to believe in

something bigger,

a God.

I wanted to believe in you

but every time

Papa praised your name

with one hand and

beat me with the other.

My older sisters,

my own mother

watched.

Did nothing.

He

just

beat

me.

No one else.

Why me?

I cried out your name,

Krishna save me.

Someone help me.

And for that he beat me more.

The things he did to me.

I learned to rely on no one.

Not God.

Not even my own family.

They left me before I left them.

So now my daughter is having you

as an invisible friend.

Karma, huh?

I pass on these stories,

not for her to believe they are real,

not for her to believe in you,

but for her to believe in herself,

believe that she can do anything she wants.

So give me something, please.

Because right now,

I can't tell that there is

anything left worth

believing in.

Painting Angels

Jane Yolen

> "For every locomotive they build,
> I shall paint another angel."
> —*Edward Burne-Jones*

For every bomb, every frack,
every drill that pierces the planet's heart,
for every spew of auto carbons,
every stealth plane mounting the sky,
every coal mine scarring a mountain,
I shall write a poem.

For every child dying in a war zone,
every infant left on a doorstep,
every child raped in the nighttime,
or kept in a cupboard, a valise, a small room,
for every child who wakes frightened,
who sleeps unfed, uncared for,
I shall write a poem.

In this world there is no end of weeping,
no end of sorrow, no end of pain,
and now there will be no end of poems.

The Escape Artist
Kevin Young

beyond the people
swallowing fire   past the other acts
we had seen before   we found the escape
artist bound to a chair   hands tied
behind his back   we climbed onstage
to test the chains   around his ankles
and tongue   watched on
as they tucked him   in a burlap sack
and lowered it   into a tank of water
he could get out of   in his sleep

imagine the air   the thin
man   his skin a drum   drawn
across bones   picture disappearing
acts   the vanishing middles
of folks from each town
the man who unsaws them
back together again   dream
each escape   is this easy   that all
you need   is a world full of walls
beardless ladies   and peeling white
fences that trap the yard   that neighbors
sink their share of ships over sketch
each side gate   the dirt roads leading
out of town   the dust that holds
no magic   here your feet are locked
to the land   to its unpicked

fields   full of empty
bags of cotton   that no one
ever seems   to work
his way out of
after the hands
on the clock met seven
times in   prayer   they drew
the artist up   unfolded his cold
body from the sack and planted
it quietly   on the way out
of town   at home we still hear
his ghost nights guess he got free
from under the red earth   but what
no one ever asked   is why
anyone would want to

What Helps

Group Poem by The Wendell B. Patrick Fun(k)ology Hour

Baseball

Water

Fuzzy-faced kittens giving whisker tickles

To talk about it

Breathing in the new, exhaling the old

The shiver of a crescent moon

Music

The unexpected "just because" call from a friend

Dancing the samba

Bean soup

The feel of a cool breeze on a silent night

The twinkling of stars

A steaming hot bath overloaded with scented bubbles

Someone standing up for you when

you're in a fight or against the wall

The feel of a canoe cutting through evening water

Purple polka dots

Long bike rides on hot summer nights

Lavender lotion

Your dog waiting at the door

Notes on Contributors

Imali Abala was born in Western Kenya and is currently living in Ohio. Her publications include *Drum Bits of Terror (2014), A Fallen Citadel* (poetry, 2012), *The Dilemma of Jahenda, the Teenage Mother* (2010), *The Disinherited* (2007) and *Move on, Trufosa* (2006). Some of her other works have appeared in *A Thousand Voices Rising,* and *Reflections: An Anthology of African Women Poets* (2013).

Faye Adams is an award-winning writer of poetry, children's books, nonfiction, and short fiction. She has been published in poetry journals and anthologies in the US, UK, Korea and Canada. Faye served as Missouri's senior poet laureate. View her work at www.fayeadams.com.

Onleilove Alston is a graduate of the Master of Divinity/Master of Social Work program at Union Theological Seminary and Columbia University School of Social Work. As a member of the Poverty Initiative she co-developed the Mary Magdala Welfare Queen Project. Onleilove is a contributing writer for *Sojourners Magazine* and Blogging Specialist at Ecumenical Women at the United Nations. She lives in New York City.

Julia Alvarez is a Dominican-American poet, novelist and essayist, author of the novel, *How the Garcia Girls Lost Their Accents* and the poetry collections, *Homecoming: New and Selected Poems* and *The Woman I Kept to Myself.* She has received grants from the National Endowment of the Arts and the Ingraham Foundation. She is the writer in residence at Middlebury College, Vermont.

Elvis Alves has written poetry that has appeared in *The Caribbean Writer's Journal, Colere, Magazine De L Mancha, First Reads, St Somewhere Journal, The Shine Journal* and *Small Axe Salon.* He lives and works in New York City.

Bobbi Arduini hold an MFA in Creative Nonfiction from St. Mary's College where she received the Chester Aaron Scholarship for excellence in writing. Her work has appeared in *Women Reinvented, Good Dogs Doing Good,* and *Sacred Fools.* She also makes music and teaches high school English. She lives in Santa Monica, California.

Cynthia Aretz, who died in 2012, lived in public housing in Minneapolis.

Peggy Aylsworth's poetry has appeared in *Beloit Poetry Journal, The Alembic, The MacGuffin, Ars Interpres (Sweden), Chiron Review, Rattle, Poetry Saltzburg Review* and numerous other journals in the United States and abroad. She was nominated for a Pushcart Prize in 2012. A retired psychotherapist, she lives in Santa Monica, California.

J. Reed Banks is an artist and a retired administrator of services for the mentally challenged in Albemarle County, Virginia. He lives in Charlottesville, Virginia.

Melissa Barber, a native of the Bronx, New York, is a single mother of an autistic daughter, and recently weathered and survived the NYC homeless shelter system. She trained and graduated as a medical physician from the Latin American School of Medicine in Havana, Cuba and is currently studying for her US licensing exams.

Glenda Barrett, a native and resident of North Georgia, is an artist, poet and writer. Her work has been published widely in such places as *Woman's World, Farm and Ranch Living, Country Woman, Chicken Soup for the Soul,* and *Journal of Kentucky Studies.* Her first chapbook was published by Finishing Line Press.

Allie Marini Batts came here to kick ass and chew bubblegum and she's ALL out of bubblegum. She is an alumna of New College of Florida. Her work has appeared in over 40 literary magazines. She is a research writer by day and is pursuing her MFA degree through Antioch University of Los Angeles. She calls Tallahassee home.

Starr Cummin Bright lives and works as a writer, farm manager (Pennsylvania) and director of a youth sailing program (Maine). She finds her way in woods, fields and on rivers and the sea, bringing physical and mystical observations to paper.

Polly Brody is the author of four books: *Other Nations, The Burning Bush, At the Flower's Lip, Stirring Shadows. At the Flower's Lip* was nominated for a Pushcart Prize. Polly's other métier is environmentalist/birder. As Chairwoman of the Newtown Conservation Commission she was instrumental in conserving a 790-acre peninsula as a CT State Forest. She lives in Southbury, CT.

Ashley Bryan is a renowned illustrator and author of numerous children's books including *Sing to the Sun, Beautiful Blackbird, The Dancing Granny, The ABCs of African-American Poetry,* and his autobiography, *Words to My Life's Song*. He has twice won the Coretta Scott King Award and won the Laura Ingalls Wilder Lifetime Achievement award. He lives on an island in Maine.

Deborah Byrne is retired from the field of Special Education and Culinary Arts and Hospitality. After a divorce, she was unable to find affordable housing while completing her degree in the Boston area. Homeless for a year, she has published poetry, photography, and articles on how poverty affects survivors of abuse. She lives in Wyoming.

Lydia Caros is a pediatrician working with Native Americans in Minneapolis, Minnesota. She is a member of the Twin Cities Friends Meeting.

Deborah Brody Chen, who writes under the name, miaokuancha, has lived long enough that it won't fit into a nutshell. New England, Taiwan, and Hawaii have all been called home. If it catches her eye or her heart it will probably end up in ink or pixels. She mothers. She nurses. She teaches. She writes. She feels. She sees. She is.

Sharon Chmielarz has had seven books of poetry published including *Calling,* a finalist for the Indie Book Awards, 2011, and *The Other Mozart.* Her most recent book is *Love From the Yellowstone Trail.* She's had poems published in magazines like *Notre Dame Review, The Iowa Review, Salmagundi, North American Review* and *Prairie Schooner.* She was awarded the *Water-Stone Review*'s 2012 Jane Kenyon Prize.

Jayne Cortez, who died in 2012, was a performance poet and jazz musician whose work was marked by outrage and protest. She founded the Watts Repertory Company and lived in New York and Senegal at the time of her death. Winner of an American Book Award, she received many fellowships including one from the National Endowment for the Arts.

Mary Cowette is an artist and a writer. She is a single mom and lives in Saint Paul, Minnesota with her kids and cats.

Stanley Crouch is a poet, essayist, musician, jazz critic and syndicated columnist for the *New York Daily News.* Two of his books have been nominated for a National Book Critics Circle Award. He is a recipient of the McArthur and Guggenheim grants. He grew up in Los Angeles and now lives in New York.

Brian Daldorph teaches at the University of Kansas and Douglas County Jail. He edits *Coal City Review.* His most recent books of poetry are *From the Inside Out: Sonnets* (Woodley Publishers, 2008) and *Jail Time* (Original Plus Publishers, 2009).

Ungelbah Daniel-Davila earned a BFA from the Institute of American Indian Art in Santa Fe, NM. Her lineage can be traced to the outlaws of the American West, the Spanish land-grant people, and the Ashihi clan of the Dine. She is the recipient of the Truman Capote Scholarship and is the creator and editor of the on line publication *La Loca Magazine.*

Ann Marie Davis is a life-long resident of the San Francisco Bay Area. In 2009, after sustaining a job-related injury, she decided to spend her life pursuing a creative path. Today, she is a writer, painter and poet and is working on her first novel tentatively titled *You Were Always Waiting for This Moment,* as well as her first collection of poetry.

Margo Davis's poetry has appeared in *Texas Poetry Calendar, New Orleans Review, Maple Leaf Rag, Passages North, The Louisville Review, Negative Capability* and *Louisiana Literature.* More recent poems appear in *Surrounded: Living with Islands, The Sow's Ear Poetry Review* and *Calliop*e. She manages Library Services at a leading law firm in Houston, Texas.

Mary Krane Derr is a poet, writer, musician and fourth generation South Side Chicagoan. Her poetry has been nominated for a Best of the Web award, *Best American Poetry,* and *Best Spiritual Writing.* She has contributed to literary magazines in the United States, Ireland, Great Britain, and India as well as anthologies like *Hunger Enough: Living Spiritually in a Consumer Society* (Pudding House).

Heid Erdrich, a member of the Turtle Mountain Band of Ojibway, serves as a visiting writer at colleges and universities around the country. She is the author of the poetry collections *Fishing for Myth* (1997), *National Monuments* (2008), and *Cell Traffic* (2012). She also authored *The Mother's Tongue* and co-edited *Sister Nations: Native American Women on Community.* She lives in Minneapolis.

Martin Espada has been called "the Latino poet of his generation." Puerto Rico is often a theme in his work. He has published 15 books of poetry which have received numerous awards, including an American Book Award. Born in Brooklyn, New York, Espada now lives in Amherst, Massachusetts where he is a professor at the University of Massachusetts.

Mike Essig was a poet, writer, teacher, tutor, and gardener who lived in Mechanicsburg, PA. He died in 2013.

Amendu Evans has served as a member of the Philadelphia's Media Mobilizing Project's Executive Committee and Labor Committee, as a site organizer for the MMP and Logan CDC Carlton Simmons Technology Keyspot Computer Center, and the coordinator of MMP's Labor Justice Radio. A hip-hop artist, stand-up comic, lifetime resident of Philadelphia, he is also a shop steward representing maintenance workers.

Patricia Fargnoli is an award winning poet and retired psychotherapist. Author of six poetry collections, including *Lives of Others, Duties of the Spirit,* and *Winter,* she was New Hampshire's poet laureate from 2006-2009. She is the recipient of a Macdowell Colony fellowship. Her poems have appeared in *Poetry, Ploughshares, Prairie Schooner, The Indiana Review, Nimrod,* and others.

Ann Filemyr is a poet and writer who serves as the Academic Dean at the Institute of American Indian Arts in Santa Fe. Her recent books of poetry include: *On the Nature of Tides* (LaNana Creek Press 2012); *The Healer's Diary* (Sunstone Press 2012); *Growing Paradise* (LaNana Creek Press 2011), and *Love Enough* (Red Mountain Press, 2013). She believes in the power of creativity to transform our lives.

Deborah Finklestein has an MFA in Creative Writing from Goddard College. Her poetry has been published in anthologies, literary magazines, and newspapers in Australia, Canada, Japan, New Zealand, Serbia and the United States, as well as in online publications. She teaches creative writing in Boston, Massachusetts.

Patricia Frisella, past President of the Poetry Society of New Hampshire, has a collection of poems published most recently in *Liberation Poetry: An Anthology,* edited by Tontongi and Jill Netchinsky (Trilingual Press, 2011). She won the 2012 International Merit Reward from *Atlanta Review.*

Brendan Galvin is the author of 12 collections of poetry including, *Atlantic Flyway*, *Hotel Malabar* (Iowa Poetry Prize), *Habitat* (National Book Award Nominee), and *Ocean Effects*. Other awards and prizes include two NEA fellowships, a Guggenheim Fellowship, The Sotheby Prize, and *Poetry's* Levinson Prize. Retired from 40 years of college teaching, he lives in Truro, Massachusetts.

Michael Glaser served as Poet Laureate of Maryland from 2004-2009 and is Professor Emeritus of St. Mary's College in St. Mary's City, Maryland. Over 500 of his poems have been published in magazines and journals. His most recent collections of poetry include: *Being a Father* (2004), *Fire Before the Hands* (Anabiosis Press, 2007), *Remembering Eden* (Finishing Line Press, 2008), and *Disrupting Consensus* (The Teacher's Voice, 2009).

David Groulx was raised in the Northern Ontario mining community of Elliot Lake. He studied creative writing at the En'owkin Centre, BC, where he won the Simon J. Lucas Jr. Memorial Award for poetry, and was a co-winner at Harbourfront Centre's 2011 PoetryNOW competition. He has written three books of poetry–*Night in the Exude*, *The Long Dance* and *Until The Bullets Rose*.

Meri Harary is an MFA candidate at Southern Connecticut State University. She received the Leo Conellan Award from the Connecticut State Arts Board and is working on her third chapbook.

Markita Hawkins is a resident of Nicollet Square, a Beacon Foundation housing project for formerly homeless youth in Minneapolis, Minnesota.

Roberta Hill is an enrolled member of the Oneida Nation of Wisconsin. A poet, fiction writer and scholar, she has been published in anthologies such as *Sing: Poetry from the Indigenous Americas* (Sun Tracks, 2011*)*, and *Bringing Gifts, Bringing News* (DownStairs Press, 2011). Her poetry collections have been *Star Quilt* (1984), *Philadelphia Flowers* (1996) and

Cicadas (2013). She is a professor in the English department and the American Indian Studies Program of University of Wisconsin, Madison.

Tanya Hough is a member of Poor Voices United. Poor Voices United, located in the Atlantic City area, is working to end poverty by uniting poor people through stories, service, advocacy and action. They help fight for the human rights to housing, health care, a living wage, education and food.

Scott Hutchison's work has appeared in numerous publications, with new work forthcoming in *The Medulla Review, The Coe Review*, and *The Tulane Review*. He is poet laureate of Gilford, New Hampshire.

Zehra Imam is currently a high school teacher in the South Bronx. Zehra is an alumna of the University of Michigan-Dearborn, and is the founder/ director for the Illuminated Cities Project, an interfaith, multi-racial experiential learning fellowship for student leaders in segregated cities.

Jim Johnson's poetry is closely tied to his roots in Northern Minnesota and reveals concern for the environment and the people and creatures in it. His books include *Finns in Minnesota Winter, A Field Guide to Blueberries*, and *Wolves*. His books *Dovetailed Corners* and *The Coop Label* were in collaboration with photographer Marlene Wisuri. He has taught in Duluth, Minnesota public schools. He was appointed Duluth Poet Laureate (2014-2016).

Lisa Kang has an MFA from Lindenwood University in Saint Charles, Missouri. She teaches Chinese and Asian Philosophy at universities and community colleges in the Saint Louis area. Her poetry has appeared *in Earth's Daughters, Calliope, Hayden's Ferry, Spillway, Greatest Uncommon Denominator* and *The View from Here.*

Kathryn Kerr is the author of four chapbooks, most recently *Turtles All the Way Down* from Finishing Line Press. Recent poems are in *Big Muddy:*

A Journal of the Mississippi Valley, Illinois English Bulletin, WordRiver, Earth's Daughters, Interdisciplinary Studies in Literature and the Environment, and Blue Line. She teaches at Illinois State University.

Susan Deborah King is the author of five collections of poetry including, *Coven, One-Breasted Woman, Bog Orchids*, and *Dropping into the Flower*. Her poems have appeared in numerous publications including *Tar River Poetry, Prairie Schooner,* and *The Willow Review*. She teaches creative writing and leads retreats on spirituality and creativity in Minneapolis and Maine.

Jonathan Langley is a poet living in the United States.

Luis Larin is a leadership organizer for The United Workers, a human rights organization in the Baltimore, MD area, led by low-wage workers who are leading the fight for fair development, which respects human rights, maximizes public benefits and is sustainable.

James P. Lenfestey is a former editorial writer for the Minneapolis *Star-Tribune*, where he won several Page One Awards for excellence. Since 2000, he has published a collection of essays, five collections of poems, a poetry anthology and co-edited *Robert Bly in This World*, University of Minnesota Press. He lives in Minneapolis with his wife of 47 years, the political activist Susan Lenfestey. They have four children and seven grandchildren.

Roseann Lloyd is the author of eight books, including three collections of poetry *Tap Dancing with Big Mom, War Baby Express, Because of the Light* and *The Boy who Slept Under the Stars*. She teaches at the Loft Literary Center in Minneapolis and is an adjunct professor at several Twin Cities colleges and universities.

George Ella Lyon is the author of thirty-five books for children and adults. Her books of poetry are *Catalpa* and *Where I'm From, Where Poems*

Come From. Recent books include *Don't You Remember?*, a memoir and *Sonny's House of Spies,* a novel for young readers. She lives in Lexington, Kentucky and works as a freelance writer and teacher.

Chosen Lyric is a poet, blogger, artist residing in Coram, New York and Port St. Lucie, Florida. He has been published in *Visions, Voices, Verses, Bards Annual 2012* and *2013, Songs of Sandy, Poetry Path* and other anthologies. His main inspiration is watching friends struggle and sometimes die from addiction. He currently specializes in storytelling poetry related to addiction.

Mekeel McBride has published six books of poetry, all from Carnegie Mellon University Press, including her latest book, *Dog Star Delicatessen, New and Selected Poems 1970-2006.* She has held fellowships at the Radcliffe Institute for Advanced Study, Princeton University, and the McDowell Colony, as well as being a recipient of two NEA grants. Her poems have appeared in the *New Yorker, Poetry, Virginia Quarterly Review, Ploughshares,* the *Georgia Review,* and many other places. She teaches at the University of New Hampshire.

Anne McCrady's writing appears in her own poetry collections, as well as literary journals, arts magazines and anthologies. She is a frequent literary and motivational speaker and advocate for peace and social justice. Her outreach includes social media and her website, InSpiritry.com. She lives in Tyler, Texas.

Ethna McKiernan is the author of three books of poems, the most recent of which *Sky Thick with Fireflies* (Salmon Poetry, Ireland). Poems of hers appear in *The Notre Dame Anthology of Irish-American Poetry, 33 Minnesota Poets* and *Beloved on the Earth.* She is employed in a non-profit working with the long-term homeless population in Saint Paul, Minnesota.

Wesley McNair is the poet laureate of Maine and emeritus professor and writer-in-residence at the University of Maine in Farmington. Winner of many fellowships, including the Rockefeller, the Guggenheim, and the National Endowment for the Arts, he is the author of nine books of poetry, the latest of which is *Lovers of the Lost*. Three collections of prose include a recent memoir, *The Words I Chose*.

Marsha Mathews is an author and educator, and a former United Methodist minister. She has published two chapbooks: *Sunglow & A Tuft of Nottingham Lace* (Red Berry Editions, 2011) and *Northbound* (Finishing Line Press). Poems of hers have appeared in *Kansas Quarterly, Inkwell, Apalachee Review,* among others. She teaches writing at Dalton State College, Dalton, Georgia.

Stephen Mead, a resident of Albany, New York is a published artist, writer and maker of short collage-films. His latest project, a collaboration with Kevin McLeod, is entitled "Whispers of Arias," a two volume CD set of narrative poems set to music.

Marsha Mentzer lives in Carlisle, PA and taught English for thirty-five years at Carlisle High School. Her poetry has been published in *Main Channel Voices, Four and Twenty, Ruminate, Relief, Tipton Poetry Journal, Caesura, Hospital Drive, Peeks and Valleys, The Village Pariah, Horticulture, Time to Sing, Seeding the Snow, Pedestal,* and *Broken Circles.*

Afzal Moolla was born in Delhi, India where his South African parents were in exile, working in the African National Congress (ANC) in the struggle against Apartheid in South Africa. Afzal currently works and lives in Johannesburg, South Africa.

Sharon Lack Munson is the author of the chapbook, *Stillness Settles Down the Lane* (Uttered Chaos Press, 2010) and a full length book of poems, *That Certain Blue.* She publishes widely in literary journals and anthologies and lives in Eugene, Oregon.

Sheryl L. Nelms is from Marysville, Kansas. An Alumna of South Dakota

State University with a concentration in Family Relations and Child Development, she has had over 5,000 articles, stories and poems published, including fourteen individual collections of poems. She is the fiction/nonfiction editor of *The Pen Woman Magazine*, and a Pushcart Prize nominee.

Marilyn Nelson is a three-time National Book Award Finalist in poetry. She has received The Poet's Prize, The Robert Frost Medal, a Newberry Honor, and three Coretta Scott King Awards. Her books include *A Wreath for Emmet Till, Carver, Fields of Praise, Faster than Light,* and, most recently, *How I Discovered Poetry*. She is emerita professor of English from the University of Connecticut.

Kara Newhouse works as a journalist and is an organizer with Put People First! PA, which fights for human rights of all people. She grew up in Millersville, PA and now lives in Duncannon.

Grace Nichols was born in Georgetown, Guyana and lived there until immigrating to the United Kingdom in 1977. Her poetry has received many awards including the Commonwealth Award for *I is a Long-Memoried Woman*. Much of her work is marked by Caribbean rhythms. She has written many books of poetry for children. She lives in East Sussex.

Naomi Shihab Nye was born to a Palestinian father and an American mother. She is the recipient of many honors and awards, among them are four Pushcart Prizes, the Jane Addams Children's Book Award and the Paterson Poetry Prize. Her books include, *Fuel, Nineteen Varieties of Gazelle, A Maze Me,* and *Transfer*.

Molly O'Dell is a practicing physician, Alegent Health Medical Director for Healthier Communities, and Adjunct Assistant Professor of Public Health and Pediatrics at the University of Nebraska Medical Center. Molly, originally from Roanoke, Virginia, completed her MFA in poetry in 2008 at University of Nebraska and has poems in *Chest, JAMA* and other journals.

Carl Palmer, twice nominated for the Micro Award and thrice for the Pushcart Prize by poetry magazine editors, is from Old Mill Rd in Ridgeway, Virginia. He now lives in University Place, Washington.

Pit Menousek Pinegar is a writer, teacher, photographer, and creative life consultant. She is the author of several books of poems, the most recent is *The Physics of Transmigration* and a book of stories entitled *Mess*. She has won numerous prizes and been offered many residencies to do her work, notably in Santa Fe, New Mexico and The Azores Islands. She lives in Middletown, CT.

Martha Postlethwaite is a minister in the United Methodist Church. Formerly chaplain of United Theological Seminary of the Twin Cities, she is now serving a recovery congregation in Saint Paul. She is also a teacher, retreat leader and writer whose pieces have been published in many periodicals and anthologies.

David Radavich is a socially committed poet, playwright, and essayist. His poetry collections have been *Slain Species* (Court Poetry, London, 1980), *By the Way* (Buttonwood 1998), *Greatest Hits* (2000) and *The Countries We Live In* (2014). He was 2009 distinguished professor at Eastern Illinois University. He lives in Charlotte, North Carolina.

Carlos Reyes lives and works in Portland, Oregon. He has read his poetry around the world from India to Ecuador, Ireland to Panama. He has received the Heinrich Boll Fellowship, a fellowship at Yaddo and the Fundacion Valparaiso (Mojacar, Spain). *The Book of Shadows: New and Selected Poems* was published in 2009 and *Pomegranate, Sister of the Heart* in 2011.

Lola Rodriguez is an award-winning New York City writer and performer whose essays, poetry, and prose have appeared in numerous anthologies and journals including *The Coffeehouse Poetry Anthology, The Evergreen Review,* et al., and is the author of several collections including, *Notes from a Solitary Rhumba.* Rodriguez has showcased her work at venues worldwide including London's Institute of Contemporary Art, The Whitney

Museum of American Art, The National Arts Club, The Literary Life with George Plimpton, The Smithsonian Institution, and many others. Once, a young runaway, she is now an educator, gadfly, scholar, and activist.

Pattiann Rogers has published eleven books of poetry and two collections essays. Her most recent collection of poems is *Holy Heathen Rhapsody*. *Firekeeper: New & Selected Poems* was a finalist for the Lenore Marshall Prize. Rogers has received two NEA grants, a Lannan Literary Award, a Guggenheim Fellowship and five Pushcart Prizes. She lives in Colorado with her husband, a geophysicist, is the mother of two sons and three grandsons.

Abigail Rome is a writer, bicyclist, conservationist and ecotourism operator with ambition to ensure the long-term health and prosperity of the earth's ecosystems. She is much more compassionate for the world around her than she was decades ago. She lives in Silver Spring, Maryland.

Helen Klein Ross is a former creative director at top ad agencies in New York who spent over 20 years in the ad business before turning to other kinds of fiction. Her stories, poems and essays have been published by the *New York Times, Los Angeles Times* and *The New Yorker*. Her first book is a coming-of-middle age story about a woman and a business (advertising).

Rose Schwab is an MDiv graduate of Union Theological Seminary in New York and a Work Study Fellow with the Poverty Initiative. She is seminarian in residence at First Unitarian Universalist Congregation of Brooklyn and hails from Saint Paul, Minnesota.

Karen Seay is settling into the idea of writing seriously after a lifetime of resisting the call. A native of South Carolina, she has made her home in Minneapolis for more than 40 years. She has taught and directed high school theatre in public schools and has practiced law. She lives with her husband Ted Allen; they have one daughter, Emilia.

Anne Eleanor Seltz writes to figure out something or just when she has figured it out. Her profession of audiology has gifted her with the opportunity to talk with thousands of people over the last 45 years about their trouble communicating. Her book about her experiences is entitled *What?*

Gene Severson attended the University of Minnesota with an interest in architecture. He has worked in mental health human services and contends with Aspberger's. After a period of homelessness, he resides at Lydia Apartments in Minneapolis where he is part of the writer's group and performs his work at various functions.

Betsy Sholl is the author of eight volumes of poetry, most recently, *Otherwise Unseeable* (University of Wisconsin, 2014). She teaches in the Vermont College of Fine Arts MFA in Writing Program, and lives in Portland, Maine. She was Poet Laureate of Maine from 2006 to 2011.

Michael Shorb is a San Francisco-based poet whose work reflects an abiding interest in environmental issues, history and the lyrical form. His poems have appeared in over 100 magazines and anthologies including *The Nation, The Sun, Michigan Quarterly Review, Queen's Quarterly, Commonweal* and *Rattle*. His collection *Whale Watcher's Morning* came out in 2013.

Marty Silverthorne lives in Greenville, North Carolina. He received the Sam Ragan Fine Arts Award in 1993 and has been awarded several grants from the North Carolina Arts Council. His poems have appeared in *The St. Andrews Review, Carolina Literary Companion, Tar River Poetry, Chattahoochee* and others. He has published two chapbooks: *Dry-Skin Messiah* and *Pot Liquor Promises*.

Claudia Solotaroff was raised in Southern Minnesota and now lives in Minneapolis. She attended the University of Minnesota and lived in Oregon for a while. She has had many different kinds of jobs and is married with three stepchildren and one daughter.

Susan Marie Swanson is an author of numerous books for children including *Getting Used to the Dark, The First Thing My Mama Told Me, Letter to the Lake* and *The House in the Night*t, which received a Minnesota Book Award and the Caldecott Medal. She teaches in the COMPAS poets-in-the-schools program and lives in Saint Paul, Minnesota.

Aaron Stauffer is a third year MDiv student at Union Theological Seminary, New York, and Associate Director, Religions for Peace, USA.

Madreen Stevens struggled with drug addiction which led to homelessness, but is now in recovery. She makes jewelry and is part of the Chicago/Franklin Arts Collective in Minneapolis. Her work appears in *Other Voice,* an anthology published by the collective.

Tony Stoneburner (b. New York City, 1926), whose BD (Drew, 1950) led him to a decade as a Methodist parish & campus minister in the Midwest & whose PhD (University of Michigan, 1966) led him to a quarter of a century as an academic in Ohio, summers in Maine & winters in Minnesota. *Gatherings & Aftermaths* (Limekiln Press, 2006) offers a selection of his poems.

Tiffany Tate is happiest when working on or near the ocean. She has worked as a lobster fisherman, a clam digger, and a boat builder. She also sings, paints and writes on an island off the coast of Maine.

John Thiemeyer was homeless for two decades and got help in Portland, OR where he found subsidized housing and medical coverage. Since finding housing he has written for a bi-weekly publication, *street roots,* whose focus is homelessness, thus advocating for those still on the street

Kim Tran is currently a graduate student in the Ethnic Studies Program at the University of California, Berkeley. She is originally from San Jose, daughter of a single mother. She has been working with her community of low-income and queer youth and hopes to teach in California public schools.

Natasha Trethewey is a former United States poet laureate. She has won a Pulitzer Prize, a Bunting Fellowship and a Guggenheim Fellowship, among other honors. Her books have been *Domestic Work, Native Guard, Bellocq's Ophelia* and *Thrall*. She is a professor of English at Emory University in Atlanta.

Connie Walle is a life-long resident of Tacoma, Washington. She is president of the Puget Sound Poetry Connection, which she founded 25 years ago. Having published over 100 poems, she founded Our Own Words, a county-wide teen writing contest in its 18th year.

Beverly Welch is the facilitator of the Lydia Apartments writer's group. She grew up on a farm west of Minneapolis and moved to Minneapolis to go to school and work. She has worked as a pre-school teacher, a journalist and as a volunteer coordinator. She has been the editor of the literary journal, *Other Voices*. Her poetry has been published in *eXpressions Journal, Full Circle, the Southwest Journal* and others and has published two books of poetry and one novel.

Colleen Wessel-McCoy has been involved with the Poverty Initiative since 2004 and currently serves as the Fellows Program Coordinator. Originally from Georgia, Colleen is a PhD candidate in Christian Social Ethics at Union Theological Seminary in New York.

John Wessel-McCoy is a project organizer at the Poverty Initiative. He is originally from Decatur, Illinois. He earned an MA from Union Theological Seminary and was awarded the Charles Augustus Briggs Award. Prior to entering the MA program at Union Theological and working with the Poverty Initiative, he was a union organizer.

Dan Williams is a poet of the Sierra Nevada mountains whose work has appeared in many journals, magazines and anthologies.

Tony Voss Williams, also known as Tony the Scribe, is a rapper and college student based in Minneapolis, MN. He is the lyricist half of the group KILLSTREAK, who put out their debut album, "Janus" in July, 2013. You can learn more about KILLSTREAK at www.killstreak.info

Keith Wilson, who died in 2009, was the author of over 40 volumes of poetry. He was the winner of many awards, including a National Endowment for the Arts Fellowship and a PEN center award. His book, *Graves Registry,* was nominated for a National Book Award in 1992. At the time of his death, he was the poet laureate of Las Cruces, New Mexico.

Laura Madeline Wiseman has a doctorate from the University of Nebraska-Lincoln where she teaches English. She is the author of five chapbooks including *Branding Girls* (Finishing Line Press 2011). Her poetry, prose and reviews have appeared in *Cream City Review, 13th Moon, Prairie Schooner, Blackbird, Mississippi Review* and others.

Carolyne Wright has published nine books and chapbooks of poetry, and four volumes of translation from Spanish and Bengali. Her books include *Mania Klepto: the Book of Eulene,* and *Seasons of Mangoes and Brainfire,* which won the American Book Award. She teaches for the Northwest Institute of Literary Arts' Whidbey Writers Workshop MFA Program and lives in Seattle.

Pam Wynn is a poet who teaches poetry and creative, liturgical, and expository writing at United Theological Seminary in New Brighton, MN. Author of *Diamonds on the Back of a Snake,* she has published widely and received support for her work from the Dayton Hudson, Jerome, and General Mills Foundations, and others. She has completed a libretto for an opera based on the book of Ruth in collaboration with composer Barbara Rogers, which was first performed in April, 2008.

Anu Yadav is a dramatist and actor. Much of her work incorporates a social justice component into the theatrical setting. '*Capers* is a solo play she developed based on the stories of D.C. public housing families who protested the demolition of their community. In addition to spearheading *Classlines*, a storytelling project about wealth and poverty, Yadav earned fellowships to train at Augusto Boal's Center for the Theatre of the Oppressed in Rio de Janeiro and to work with the Indian street theater troupe, Jana Natya Manch, in New Delhi. She lives in Washington, D.C.

Jane Yolen is the author of over 340 books, including *Owl Moon* and *The Devil's Arithmetic*. Her books and stories have won two Nebula Awards, A World Fantasy Award, a Caldecott, the Golden Kite Award, three Mythopoetic awards, two Christopher Medals, a nomination for the National Book Award, and many others. She divides her time between Massachusetts and Scotland.

Kevin Young is a professor of English and Creative Writing at Emory University and the author of several collections of poetry including *Ardency, Dear Darkness, For the Confederate Dead* and *Jazz Poems*. He has won the PEN/Open Book award, The Quill award and the Patterson Poetry Prize. He was raised mostly in Topeka, Kansas and lives now in Atlanta, Georgia.

Permissions and Sources

We wish to express our thanks to authors, editors and publishers and other copyright holders for their permission to include the works indicated below.

"Spic" by Julia Alvarez originally appeared in *The Woman I Kept to Myself* (Algonquin, 2004) and reprinted by permission.

"Ursus Horribilis" by Polly Brody originally appeared in *Other Nations* (Wood Thrush Press) and reprinted by permission of the author.

"Song" by Ashley Bryan originally appeared in *Sing to the Sun* (Harper Collins, 1992) and reprinted by permission of the author.

"Washing My Face" by Sharon Chmielarz originally appeared in *Rhubarb King* (Loonfeather Press, 2006) and reprinted by permission of the author.

"Global Inequalities" by Jayne Cortez originally appeared in *On the Imperial Highway* (Hanging Loose Press, 2009) and reprinted by permission.

"She Was the Kind" by Heid Erdrich originally appeared in *National Monuments* (Michigan State University Press, 2008) and reprinted by permission of the author.

"My Cockroach Lover" by Martin Espada originally appeared in *Imagine the Angels of Bread* (W. W. Norton, 1996) and reprinted by permission.

"Dante's Inferno" by Patricia Fargnoli originally appeared in *Then, Something* (Tupelo Press, 2009) and reprinted by permission of the author.

"A Photo of Miners" by Brendan Galvin originally appeared in *The Minutes No One Owns* (University of Pittsburgh Press, 1978) and reprinted by permission of the author.

"Dream of Rebirth" by Roberta Hill originally appeared in *Cicadas* (Holy Cow! Press, 2013) and reprinted by permission of the author.

"from *Dovetailed Corners*" by Jim Johnson originally appeared in *Dovetailed Corners* (Holy Cow! Press, 1996) and reprinted by permission of the author.

"A Dozen Reasons to Give Up Haggling for the Price of Weavings" by Roseann Lloyd originally appeared in *Because of the Light* (Holy Cow! Press, 2002) and reprinted by permission of the author.

"Looking at a Photograph of My Mother, Age 3" by George Ella Lyon originally appeared in *Catalpa* (Wind Publications, 1993) and reprinted by permission.

"A Little Bit of Timely Advice" by Mekeel McBride, Copyright © 2001 by Mekeel McBride, originally appeared in *Dog Star Delicatessen: New and Selected Poems 1979-2006* (Carnegie Mellon, 2006) and reprinted with the permission of The Permissions Company, Inc., on behalf of Carnegie Mellon University Press, www.cmu.edu/universitypress.

"Tuesday at the Outreach Office" by Ethna McKernan originally appeared in *Sky Thick with Fireflies* (Salmon Poetry, 2011) and reprinted by permission of the author.

"After My Step Father's Death" by Wesley McNair originally appeared in *The Town of No* (Godine, 1989) and reprinted by permission of the author.

"Washboard Wizard" by Marilyn Nelson originally appeared in *Carver* (Front Street, 2001) and reprinted by permission of the author.

"Real Estate" by Naomi Shihab Nye originally appeared in *Transfer* (BOA Editions, 2012) and is reprinted by permission of the author.

About the Editor

Susan Deborah King is the author of 5 full-length collections of poetry and one chapbook, including *One-Breasted Woman* and *Dropping into the Flower*, both from Holy Cow! Press. She has taught Creative Writing at several institutions in Minneapolis, notably as artist-in-residence at United Theological Seminary. She also leads retreats on creativity and spirituality. A process she devised involving interaction with and the production of art and poetry called "Divinations" is meant to help guide individuals who are in crisis or at a crossroads. She is a graduate of Union Theological Seminary and lives in Maine. You can reach her at Samethyst@aol.com or on her website: susandeborahking.com.